The Curtain, Ben Nevis
Photo: Mungo Ross

SBN 902 363 31 X

First Edition (by I.S.Clough) March 1969
Reprinted April 1969, April 1970
Second Edition (Revised by H.MacInnes) March 1974
Reprinted December 1976
Third Edition (by Ed. Grindley) February 1981
Reprinted December 1984

WINTER CLIMBS
BEN NEVIS
AND
GLENCOE

Ed. GRINDLEY

Drawings by R. B. Evans

Published by Cicerone Press
Harmony Hall, Milnthorpe, Cumbria, England

Front cover: The Screen, Aonach Dubh
Photo: Ed. Grindley.

Back cover: Buachaille Etive Mor
Photo: H.M.Brown

CONTENTS

FOREWORD

In the 11 years since the appearance of the original Clough guide, Scottish winter climbing has undergone considerable change: not only in terms of numbers of climbers but also in terms of the popularity of the hardest climbs - few routes remain unrepeated for long these days. Hence the complete update of the guide. The guide is still selective but it describes all major winter lines, although brief descriptions will still leave scope for a climber's route finding skill to be necessary. I would like to thank Mick Geddes, Con Higgins and Alan Kimber for advice and Sheana Hall and Rosemary Weir for help with typing.

Ed. Grindley 1980.

INTRODUCTION

Ben Nevis and the peaks of Glencoe give some of the finest winter mountaineering in Britain. The mountains are bigger than those of England and Wales and can generally be relied upon to retain a good covering of permanent snow from December until April or May. The original pioneers tended to regard Scottish snow climbing as good training for greater mountaineering but winter climbing as practiced today has developed into a very specialised sub-sport and many now consider that the Alps can provide useful training for Scottish ice!

Many of the longer routes are more Alpine than British in length and character but Scottish winter mountaineering can be even more serious than climbing in the Alps. The weather is often precarious and blizzards of arctic ferocity can strike with startling suddenness, transforming a pleasant excursion into a battle for survival. Too many people underestimate Scottish Mountains, too many have died. Even expert parties, climbing in perfect weather, have had their epics due to unexpected conditions high on the route. There are many embarrassing stories of famous men, Himalayan veterans too, getting themselves into trouble on Ben Nevis. One such was so impressed that he remarked that if a man could climb safely on the Ben in winter, then he could climb safely anywhere in the world. There may have been an element of rueful cynicism behind this remark for the gentleman had just broken his leg.

A combination of short daylight hours and the danger of a break in the weather gives Scottish winter climbing an alpine-like urgency. Speed is the critical factor and because of this there is no need for an artificial code of ethics such as is applied to British rock climbing. Speed is as vital as in the Alps and, although times can vary enormously according to the conditions encountered, a fast time is the criterion of ability. Conversely, a slow time is generally a sign of incompetence.

Conditions of Snow and Ice

To the winter mountaineer, a thorough knowledge of snow structure is vital. Not only does this knowledge help him to estimate avalanche risk but also enables him to select routes most likely to be in condition. The following summary may be helpful but climbers preparing for a Scottish winter holiday would be well advised to read and study **Avalanches and Snow Safety** by Colin Frazer, which gives easy reading and contains much useful information relevant to snow and ice mountaineering.

The different types of snow and ice commonly met in Britain can be very simply categorised:-

1. Fresh fallen snow.
2. Settled snow.
3. Firn snow.
4. White ice.
5. Green ice.

There are many different varieties of snow and ice in each of these general categories. Verglas is caused by raindrops falling on frozen ground and usually forms a very thin transparent veneer although it can be quite thick. Black ice is caused by the freezing of drainage water. Both these ice conditions are extremely tough and make climbing very difficult as natural holds are covered and yet the skin of ice is generally too thin to allow steps to be cut or picks to hold.

'Ideal conditions' consist of hard-packed firn snow or white ice (both commonly referred to as nevé). This is the best material for front-pointing. Unfortunately these conditions do not occur all that frequently even in Scotland and early climbers were very often frustrated. When lacking firn snow in the gullies, great sport can be had on the ridges, buttresses and faces - battling with powder snow, verglassed rocks and frozen vegetation. When spells of hard frost prevent the snows of the upper corries from consolidating, low-level water courses can provide interesting high standard climbing on brittle ice. Some of the climbs in this selection are scarcely worthy of attention if conditions are good at higher levels; they have been chosen deliberately as interesting alternatives to floundering through deep powder snow.

Avalanches

Every year deaths occur in avalanches, especially on Ben Nevis. Simple rules can lessen the risk.

1. Do not attempt to climb during or until at least 24 hrs. after a heavy snow fall.

2. Avoid gullies during periods of thaw, especially if they are known to carry large cornices. The ridges and buttresses will usually provide safer alternatives.

Apart from avalanche risk, winter mountaineers face the danger of falling rock and ice chunks often released by higher parties and sometimes loosened by sunlight. Experience and knowledge can reduce these dangers.

Equipment and safety precautions.

Ice axe and crampons are essential for any winter outing. On all but the easiest climbs it is assumed that two drooped or inclined ice tools are carried : route times are based on this assumption. Pegs and nuts must be carried for belaying - axe and ice-screws are not reliable enough to form main belays. Before being tempted to save time and effort by using an axe or screw belay consider the appalling number of deaths caused recently by total anchor failures.

Food and spare clothing should be carried but novice parties often over-estimate and carry far too much food, clothing and equipment. Remember that an unnecessarily heavy rucsac will cause tiredness and slowness.

A sound knowledge of navigation techniques is essential, learn it before you go on the winter hills and take advantage of clear days to reinforce your knowledge.

A good headtorch is a must.

Many accidents occur during the descent. Be sure you have identified the correct descent line or gully and beware of cornices. If in doubt take the long way round.

Never, never glissade unless you can see all the way down and even then remember that there may be hidden crags and ice. Consider whether the saving in effort is worth possible injury.

NOTES ON THE USE OF THE GUIDE

Gradings

The usual Scottish winter grading system is used, ranging in increasing difficulty from simple (though often steep) snow slopes at Grade I, to the hardest of modern winter routes at Grade VI. This new Grade VI is based on the assumption that the old hard classics like Point 5 and Zero represent standard Grade V in average conditions: Grade VI routes are harder and fewer parties will succeed in climbing them. Obviously the winter grade of a climb can vary enormously depending on the prevailing conditions, those given in this guide are for average conditions.

Times

A competent team should expect to beat or at least equal the ascent times given. A slow time is usually a mark of incompetence rather than a measure of poor conditions.

Recommendations

As the guide is selective, all of the climbs recorded have some merit but a star system is used as a further back-up: the more stars the better the route.

Rope length

On all but the easiest climbs double 150ft ropes should be considered essential to facilitate a possible abseil retreat.

Length of climbs

This is usually a <u>vertical height</u> rather than a summation of pitch lengths. The terms left and right apply when facing uphill.

Season

The winter season can extend from November to May but until late January one can expect a poor build-up of snow and a corresponding existence of pitches that are normally banked out later in the season.

Maps

The one-inch O.S. Tourist sheet Lorne and Lochaber covers both areas as does sheet 41 (Ben Nevis) of the newer 1:50,000 series. Either is fine and should be considered an essential piece of equipment.

Helicopter notes

Helicopters are increasingly used for rescue. If you are with the casualty, secure all loose gear and move all unnecessary people away. When the helicopter comes into view signal that you are its quarry (this can be difficult for the pilot to decide on a crowded mountain) by raising the arms in a V above the head. Have a belay ready if necessary but **DO NOT** clip the winchman in until he says so. Field the winchman (let him ground first) and steady him until he gets his bearings. He will carry first aid gear and the knowledge how to use it. If the helicopter hovers for any time above, shield the casualty from the resulting and often intense wind, cold and spindrift. Do not approach a helicopter until the pilot signals. Be aware of the main and tail rotors.

BEN NEVIS (4406ft)

ACCOMMODATION

The Charles Inglis Clark Memorial Hut is situated at 2,200ft. beneath the great cliffs of the north-east face and close to the burn in the glen of the Allt a'Mhuillinn (M.R. NN168723). It is perfectly placed just above the convergence of the two main approach tracks and at the divergence of the routes into the two corries. Its situation is magnificent and as a base from which to climb it is unrivalled in the British Isles. Owned by the Scottish Mountaineering Club, it is available to members of B.M.C. affiliated clubs but bookings should be made through club secretaries. 16 places (minimum booking 3 places). Custodian: R.T.Richardson, 2 Inchlonaig Drive, Balloch, Dunbartonshire.

The C.I.C. Hut is the ideal centre but is becoming increasingly popular and it may be impossible to secure bookings. In this event there are two reasonable alternatives:-

Glen Nevis S.Y.H.A. is situated on the south bank of the River Nevis about three miles from Fort William, at the start of one of the two main approach routes.

Steall Hut in Upper Glen Nevis (M.R. NN178684) is owned by the Lochaber M.C. and has 15 places. Bookings should be made to the Custodian: I.Walker, 12 Grange Terrace, Fort William, Inverness-shire.

Both of these are well over 2 hours from the cliffs and in order to accomplish any really worthwhile climbing one must be fit, enthusiastic and prepared to make an 'alpine' start.

The B.M.C. hut at Onich forms a reasonable base for both Glencoe and Ben Nevis.Further details from the BMC, Crawford House, Precinct Centre, Booth Street East, Manchester.

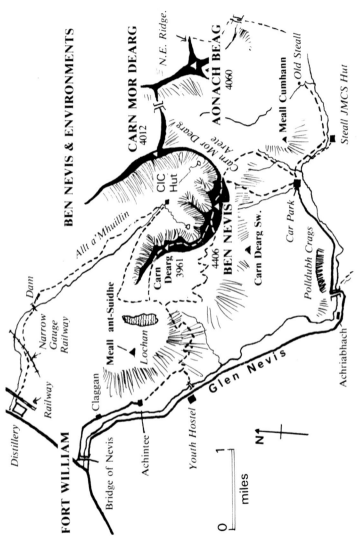

BEN NEVIS & ENVIRONMENTS

CARN MOR DEARG
4012

N.E. Ridge.

AONACH BEAG
4060

Meall Cumhann

Old Steall

Steall JMCS Hut

Carn Mor Dearg Arête

CIC Hut

Allt a'Mhuillin

Carn Dearg Sw.

Car Park

BEN NEVIS

4406

Carn Dearg
3961

Polldubh Crags

Meall ant-Suidhe

Lochan

Achriabhach

Glen Nevis

Dam

Narrow Gauge Railway

Railway

Distillery

Claggan

FORT WILLIAM

Bridge of Nevis

Achintee

Youth Hostel

N

0   1
miles

14

APPROACHES

There are two standard approaches to the C.I.C. Hut:-

1. The route from the North-West starts from the distillery near Lochy Bridge. (M.R. NN 125757). Cross the main line railway and after over half-a-mile of boggy heathland, reach another disused railway track. This is followed to the north for a few hundred yards, until after crossing a small bridge, a path leads up the slope on the right, through the trees. Above this point the path is quite steep and sometimes vague (there are two variations) but trends diagonally leftwards across the slope to meet the Allt a'Mhuillinn where it is dammed (i.e. just over the brow of the hill). Pass over the dam and continue up the glen for about three miles by a well marked track, recross the burn to link up with the other route just short of the hut and where the burn from Coire na Ciste joins the main stream. The dam can also be reached by parking at the golf club (M.R. NN137763), crossing the golf course, and walking up the east side of the stream.

This is probably the best and fastest approach. However, it is often very boggy after a thaw. In reasonable conditions and assuming that a load is carried, it should take 2-3 hours, but heavy drifted snow can make for very hard going and may double the time. In bad visibility care should be taken to avoid passing the hut and continuing up into Coire Leis.

2. The approach from the South-West follows the zig-zagging pony-track (the tourist track to the summit of the Ben) as far as the broad saddle between Meall an t-Suidhe and the main massif of Carn Dearg N.W. Ben Nevis. The pony-track starts from Achintree Farm but a popular short-cut is to cross the bridge opposite Glen Nevis Youth Hostel and climb steeply up to join the main track. Above the saddle which holds the large Lochan Meall an t-Suidhe (or 'Half-way Lochan'), the pony-track veers back to the right (south) crosses the Red Burn, and zig-zags up the long slope to the summit plateau. Where the pony track swings to the south, the route to the hut branches off northwards. It follows an indefinite path contouring the lower slopes of Carn Dearg above the Half-

way Lochan for about half a mile until it reaches the remains of an old fence on the lip of the Allt a'Mhuillinn glen. From this point it gradually descends for about 100 feet in a north-easterly direction and then continues traversing south-east across the hillside until it reaches Allt a'Mhuilinn. A large boulder, the Lunching Stone, will be seen on the left of the path along this traverse. The route now follows the right bank of the Allt a'Mhuilinn burn until it is joined by another large stream coming in from the right (out of Coire na Ciste). This is crossed, and the hut, situated on the crest of a blunt spur between the streams, is about a hundred yard above.

Starting from the Youth Hostel, this approach is only slightly longer than the route up the glen but in bad visibility the route-finding is more difficult and after a big snowfall the saddle and traverse into the glen are very prone to heavy drifting and possible avalanche below the Castle area.

3.   Other approaches to the North-east face. There are two alternative variations (with little to choose between them) starting from the large car park at the end of the Glen Nevis road. Both are exceptionally steep and are unsuitable for use as a means of reaching the C.I.C. Hut and not recommended for reaching the majority of climbs. But in good visibility for the fit valley based climber, they give the quickest approach to the Little Brenva Face or the normal route on North-east Buttress.

(a) From the car park take a diagonal line up the hillside to reach the saddle between Meall Cumhan and Ben Nevis and then follow the ridge in a north-westerly direction. Finally, when the steep ridge merges into the easier angled slopes above, veer slightly right to gain the Carn Mor Dearg Arete at the Abseil Posts. Descend by the Posts into Coire Leis. (2-2½ hrs).

(b) Climb straight up above the car park following the bank of the waterslide of Allt Coire Eoghainn. Once over the lip of the Coire, head up the right (north-east) to join the previous route on the ridge a few hundred feet below the Carn Mor Dearg Arete.

16

(c) From the Steall Hut the best way is to join route (a) at the Meall Cumhan saddle. Follow a small indefinite track which leaves upper Glen Nevis immediately above the entrance to the gorge, and makes a rising traverse above it, crossing the flank of Meall Cumhan until it is possible to strike up to the saddle. Alternatively one may follow the Allt Coire Giubhsachan (above the ruin of the old Steall) and head directly up the westward branch corrie to gain the Carn Mor Dearg Arete. However, there are great areas of slab in this corrie which can be very difficult under icy conditions.

DESCENTS

Often, particularly on Ben Nevis, the descent may call for more concentration and shrewdness of judgement than any other part of the day. The best descent will be determined not only by your point of arrival on the summit plateau but the weather and snow conditions. The shortest way will not necessarily be the best and in really bad conditions the only safe way off the mountain may be by route (a) below, long and tiresome though it may be. Careful use of map and compass and the sketch-plan of the cliffs given in this guidebook will suffice to get you down but local knowledge is invaluable. When visibility is good, make a close study of the general topography of the mountain and if possible visit the summit plateau with a view to memorising its details.

The ruined Observatory, topped by a survival shelter, is an un-mistakeable landmark on the summit itself even though the neighbouring triangulation point and numerous cairns may be obliterated in a hard winter. From the Observatory the top of the N.E.Buttress is 300 yards to the east of north and the top of Tower Ridge is 250 yards to the west; this part of the plateau is comparitively level. In order to follow the northern rim of the summit plateau, north-westwards from the Observatory, one must first move in a southerly direction to avoid the deep re-entrant of Gardyloo Gully. Shortly beyond this are the heavy cornice of Tower Gully and then the projection on the top of Tower Ridge. Then there is a gradual swing back to the left and a steady descent to the top of No. 3 Gully and its characteristic pinnacle which divides the exit into two forks. The top of No. 3 Gully is about half-a-mile away from and 500 feet below the Observatory. Now there is a slight rise and a projection to the north. This is Creag Coire na Ciste with its three gully cornices comparitively close, the last gully, North Gully, has a pinnacle which must not be confused with the one at the top of No. 3 Gully. The slope has already begun a gradual descent before the North Gully's cornice is passed and it is only a short distance to the col between Ben Nevis and Carn Dearg N.W. and the wide fan cornice above No. 4 Gully.

This route along the cliff-tops is the most important part of any descent in bad visibility. Beyond the shallow, indefinite col, and the top of No. 4. Gully, the slope at the cliff edge rises gradually once more, swinging rightwards out over the Trident Buttress before pulling back to the head of No. 5. Gully. There is another survival shelter 200 yards from the top of No. 4 Gully on a bearing 355° (magnetic).

The following are the main routes of descent:

a) **From the summit** go to the top of Gardyloo Gully, 110 metres (2½ normal rope lengths) on magnetic 240° (in white-out conditions **stay roped** and keep one person **belayed.** Then take magnetic 290° to reach the Red Burn in about a mile. Beware of the plateau rim on the right initially, and avoid straying leftwards into the area of Five Finger Gully later on. The second bearing can be used from the top of **Tower Ridge.**

b) In good visibility follow the rim of the plateau north-westwards to Number 4 Gully which is marked by an aluminium post. Descend this - the angle soon eases and the post could always be used to fix a top rope.

(c) The descent from the Observatory to the C.M.D. Arete and thence down Coire Leis is the most treacherous on the

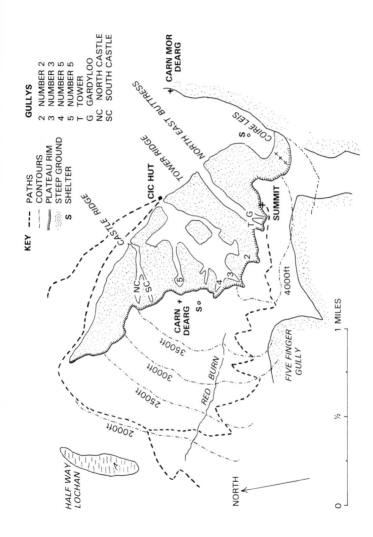

KEY --- PATHS
- ·-· CONTOURS
- ······ PLATEAU RIM
- STEEP GROUND
- **S** SHELTER

GULLYS

2 NUMBER 2
3 NUMBER 3
4 NUMBER 5
5 NUMBER 5
T TOWER
G GARDYLOO
NC NORTH CASTLE
SC SOUTH CASTLE

CARN MOR DEARG

COIRE LEIS

TOWER RIDGE

NORTH EAST BUTTRESS

CIC HUT

CASTLE RIDGE

SUMMIT

T G

NC SC

5

4

3

2

S

CARN + DEARG

4000ft

3500ft

3000ft

2500ft

RED BURN

FIVE FINGER GULLY

2000ft

HALF WAY LOCHAN

NORTH

0   ½   1 MILES

19

mountain. Despite numerous recent aids to safety it can only be recommended in good weather and even then the initial slope is often subject to very heavy icing and may require great care. Do not attempt this descent in bad visibility. From the C.M.D. Arete one may descend into Corie Leis by the line of abseil posts or reverse approach route 3 into upper Glen Nevis.

A worthwhile extension (in good weather) for parties returning to the C.I.C Hut is to follow the crescent-shaped arete to the summit of Carn Mor Dearg (4012ft.) enjoying magnificent views of the Nevis cliffs. In good conditions it is occasionally possible to glissade effortlessly from the summit for nearly 2,000 ft., almost down to the Hut. But, as always with glissading, considerable caution should be exercised.

EMERGENCIES

There is an emergency shelter 150yds. above the Lochan in Coire Leis and about 400 yds. north-east of the lowest abseil post (G.R. NN174713) like the others near the Observatory and Carn Dearg N.W. it is painted orange for easy identification. The shelters, No. 4. Gully marker and abseil posts have all been installed by the Lochaber Mountaineering club who, with the police, constitute the local rescue team. Their contributions toward accident prevention are highly commendable and it is to be hoped that the users of this guide will respect their efferts and observe every safety precaution. However genuine accidents do happen.

There are three rescue kits available, at the C.I.C. Hut, at Steall Hut and in Fort William. There is a direct phone link to the police from the C.I.C Hut.

The nearest telephones are at Glen Nevis Youth Hostel or a public telephone booth near the distillery at Lochy Bridge (the number of the police station at Fort William is 2361).

GENERAL TOPOGRAPHY

The northerly faces of Ben Nevis and Carn Dearg N.W. form one continuous complex of cliffs which attain a maximum height of 2,000ft. and extend for two miles overlooking the upper part of the Allt a'Mhuilinn glen. It is the most impressive mountain face in the British Isles. The incomparable classic ridges are flanked by formidable walls leading back into deeply recessed corries which themselves contain numerous large buttresses and gullies. The scale is so vast that it is difficult to appreciate, particularly on first acquaintance.

Walking up the glen of the Allt a'Mhuilinn, the first thing the climber will see on his right is Castle Ridge and its flanking North Wall. Beyond this and at a higher level is the recess of Castle Corrie which contains the Castle itself, its two demarcating gullies and to the left of these the tapering pillar of Raeburn's Buttress. The cliffs then jut out again. The left hand side of the Castle Corrie is known as the North Wall of Carn Dearg; this cliff connects with a 1000ft prow of compact rock, a truncated spur, the Great Buttress of Carn Dearg. Waterfall Gully is the dividing line between these last two. Round the corner of the Great Buttress is No. 5 Gully, set at a reasonable angle but almost 2,000ft in length. Ledge Route comes out of No. 5 Gully to gain the crest of the ridge at the top of the Great Buttress and follows this to the summit of Carn Dearg. To the left (east) of the Great Buttress the cliffs fall back to form the great amphitheatre of Coire na Ciste, the floor of which at over 3,000ft, is over a quarter mile wide. There are three relatively easy exits from the head of the corrie; No. 4 gully (hidden) on the right; No. 3 Gully apparently the lowest col in the centre and No. 2 Gully which disappears to the left of the prominent buttress of the Comb. Tower Ridge is the next main feature and is one of the most important on the mountain. Narrow and very long, it projects for half a mile from the summit plateau into the glen to terminate abruptly as the Douglas Boulder. From the foot of the boulder (700ft in itself!) there is a vertical rise of over 2,000ft before the junction with the plateau.

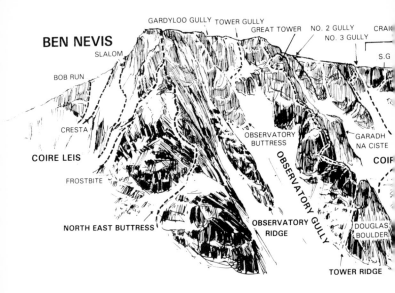

BEN NEVIS

GARDYLOO GULLY   TOWER GULLY
GREAT TOWER   NO. 2 GULLY   CRAI
NO. 3 GULLY
SLALOM
S.G
BOB RUN
CRESTA
OBSERVATORY
BUTTRESS
GARADH
NA CISTE
COIRE LEIS
COIF
FROSTBITE
OBSERVATORY GULLY
NORTH EAST BUTTRESS
OBSERVATORY
RIDGE
DOUGLAS
BOULDER
TOWER RIDGE

To the east of Tower Ridge is the long slope of Observatory Gully which branches in its upper quarter to form Gardyloo and Tower Gullies. Observatory Gully, broad in its lower part and tapering as it rises for 1,500ft is only an approach to other climbs and can be regarded almost as a deep corrie. Rising to the left of the gully are some of the most formidable climbs on the mountain: The Minus Gullies and Buttresses and the Orion Face (all on the flank of North East Buttress); Zero Gully which lies in the corner between Orion Face and the long spur of Observatory Ridge and finally Point Five Gully and Observatory Buttress.

The final great ridge almost at the head of the glen is called the North East Buttress. It is again a massive projection, almost 2,000ft in vertical height, but is steeper and therefore not as long as Tower Ridge. Below the First Platform it terminates in a great rock nose not unlike the Douglas Boulder. The Allt a'Mhuilinn glen ends in Coire Leis below

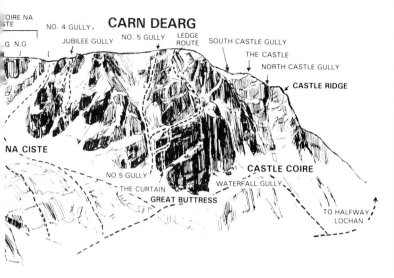

the col of the Carn Mor Dearg Arete. Overlooking this corrie is the east flank of the North East Buttress; now generally referred to as the 'Little Brenva Face'.

The climbs are described from east to west (l. to r.) corrie by corrie.

CLIMBS FROM COIRE LEIS

Coire Leis is the basin at the head of the Allt a'Mhuilinn glen. From the C.I.C. Hut follow the right bank of the burn until opposite the lowest rocks below the First Platform North East Buttress, then traverse up the r. hand side of the corrie beneath the east face (about 1 hr. from the C.I.C. Hut).

23

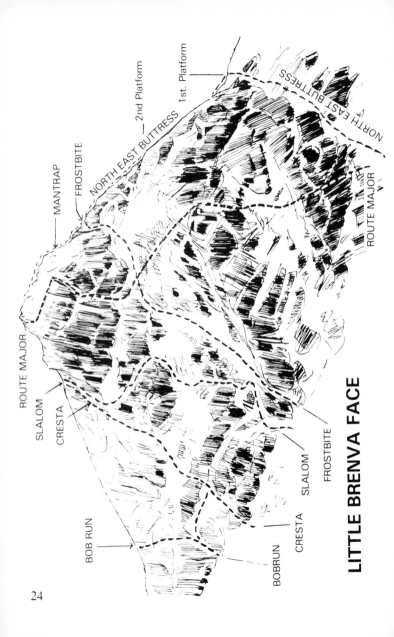

LITTLE BRENVA FACE

Althought all the routes on the Little Brenva follow fairly arbitrary lines they are very popular. The face is alpine in character, receives the full benefit of any sun and consequently often becomes heavily iced. Generally the climbs are long and give some interesting route finding; considerable difficulty may be experienced in misty conditions.

Bob-run   400ft   Grade II   1 hr.
I.Clough, D.Pipes and party.   10th February 1959.

Commences almost at the level of the col of the Carn Mor Dearg Arete and follows a couloir in the l. extremity of the face. A good introduction to the more serious routes. Start to the r. of a buttress and climb 100ft of ice or iced rocks to gain the couloir. After another 100ft the route curls round to the l. by either of two variations, both of which generally give at least one further pitch on ice.

Cresta Climb   900ft   Grade II/III**   2-3 hours.
T.W.Patey, L.S.Lovat and A.G.Nicol. 16th Feb 1957.

The main feature of this route is a 600ft shallow couloir which commences above and to the l of a 300ft rocky spur and finishes amongst the small cliffs at the exit from the highest part of the l. hand side of the face. The original start was from the r. but it is now more usual to commence to the l. of the rocky spur and about 100ft r. of Bob-run. 100ft of icy rocks (or ice) are climbed to gain a long broad snowshelf. A small gully leads up from the r. hand side of the shelf to reach the couloir proper which is followed to its termination in an ice basin. Traverse up to the r. to gain an easy snow slope which leads out to a finish about 50 yards from the top of N.E.Buttress.

Slalom   900ft   Grade II/III**   2-3 hours
D.Pipes, I.Clough, J. M.Alexander, R.Shaw and A.Flegg 6th Jan 1959.

The upper part of the r. hand side of the face is a steep rock wall, the Central Spur. Both Slalom and Frostbite start in the bay below this wall and to the r. of a 300ft. rocky spur.

Slalom starts up a shallow tongue of snow from the l. of the bay and zig-zags up through rock bluffs towards the middle of the wall of the Central Spur. Below the Spur a long rising leftwards traverse is made to gain an easy snow slope which leads to the foot of a rocky ridge overlooking the couloir of Cresta. The rocks usually give the crux of the climb and lead to the final easy exit slope which is shared with Cresta.

Frostbite 900ft Grade III 2-4hrs.
I.Clough, D.Pipes, J.M.Alexander, P.A.Hannon and M.Bucke. Feb 1958.

Starts from the above mentioned bay and follows an icy groove up to the r. to gain a 400ft snow field. Follow this rightwards and cross a rocky ridge below the nose of the Central Spur proper to gain further snowslopes slanting rightwards under the Spur. These eventually lead out onto the crest of the N.E. Buttress below the Mantrap.

Route Major 1,000ft Grade III ** 3-5hrs.
H.MacInnes and I.Clough. 16th Feb 1969.

This route follows the line of the Eastern Climb and provides one of the most enjoyable winter routes on Ben Nevis. Start from above and to the l. of North East Buttress Route and follow the ice ribs up the wall to gain a snowslope crossed by Frostbite. Cross this and continue up the buttress above by a chimney line going up and right (complicated route finding). Where the route goes close to the Mantrap, break out left on a horizontal traverse then up various small snowfields to the top.

North East Buttress 1,500ft Grade III/IV *** 2-5hrs.
First winter ascent unknown.

The normal winter route avoids the rocks below the First

Platform by going up into Coire Leis until a broad easy shelf leads back up to the r. to the First Platform. Shortly above the Platform the rocks on the crest become very steep and the easiest route is to traverse an exposed ledge on the r. until a gully leads back up to the l. to reach the small Second Platform. Alternatively the steep step may be turned on the l. or even taken direct. Above the Second Platform the ridge is followed, turning obstacles, until a smooth blunt 15ft nose bars the way. This is the notorious Man-Trap which can be extremely difficult in icy conditions. It is best turned on the r. by a slight descent and traverse to a scoop. This leads to the foot of a steep corner which again can be very hard. It may be best to move slightly down to the l. until, not far above the top of the Man-trap, a shallow chimney leads up to the l. of the ridge crest on to easier ground. This upper part of the route is normally the crux of the climb, but the major difficulties are relatively short and it is not too far to the top; probably better to force the route than be faced with the long retreat.

CLIMBS FROM OBSERVATORY GULLY

Slingsby's Chimney   400ft   Grade II   1hr.

A direct approach to the First Platform of N.E.Buttress from the west. To the r. of the slabby rocks of the nose leading to the First Platform is an obvious shallow gully fault. This gives the climb.

THE MINUS AND ORION FACES

To the r. of Slingsby's Chimney is a steep area of cliff leading to N.E. Buttress. It is split by three gullies (the Minus Gullies: Minus 3 on the left) and bounded on the right by Zero Gully. The lower part of the routes are often out of condition.

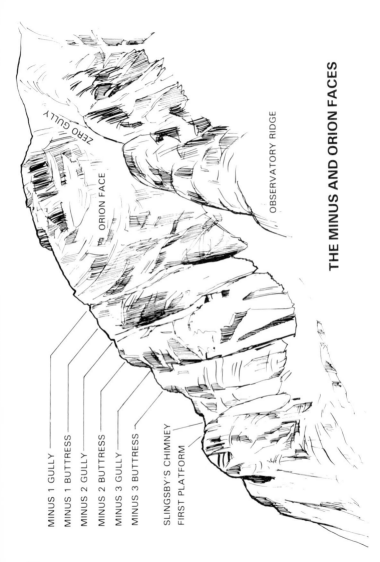

MINUS 1 GULLY
MINUS 1 BUTTRESS
MINUS 2 GULLY
MINUS 2 BUTTRESS
MINUS 3 GULLY
MINUS 3 BUTTRESS
SLINGSBY'S CHIMNEY
FIRST PLATFORM

ZERO GULLY

ORION FACE

OBSERVATORY RIDGE

THE MINUS AND ORION FACES

MINUS THREE BUTTRESS

Lies immediately to the right of Slingsby's Chimney; bounded to the right by Minus Three Gully. All routes escapable.

Right-hand Wall Route   500ft   Grade IV   2-3 hrs.
R.Ferguson and J.Higham. March, 1972.

Just to the right of Slingsby's Chimney is a line of chimneys: follow this line as close as possible, the final slabby part below the First Platform giving the crux.

Wagroochimsla   500ft   Grade IV   2-3hrs.
S.Docherty and G.Adam. January, 1972.

Start between Right-hand Wall and Platform's Rib and climb left to the central bulge; climbed on aid. Continue rightwards to the Second Platform.

Platform's Rib   700ft   Grade IV   2-3hrs.
H.MacInnes, I.Clough, T.Sullivan and M.White.
8th March, 1959.

Follow the rib to the left of Minus Three Gully until part of the gully is used before moving back left to the North East Buttress.

Minus Three Gully   600ft   Grade IV*** 2-3 hours
R.Smith and J.Marshall. 7th Feb 1960.

When in condition, a classic. Climb steep snow to a cave belay, climb steep ice on the l. and continue by a groove to snow. Another steep pitch leads to easier climbing and North East Buttress.

MINUS TWO BUTTRESS

To the right of Minus Three Gully is a slabby buttress, interrupted at about one third height by overhangs and forming a prominent ridge on the left. Bounded to the right by Minus Two Gully.

Left-hand Route   900ft*   Grade VI   8 hours.
S.Docherty and N.Muir. 30th Jan 1972.

Start immediately right of Minus Three Gully and ascend the ridge for a couple of hundred feet to an overlap. Descend a little; then swing round a rib and up a snow arete to a belay below an overhang. From a peg in the overhang tension to the slab's edge and up to belay on right wall. Steep ice leads to an easier section of slabby rocks and eventually to Second Platform.

Central Route   900ft   Grade VI   5-8 hours.
A.Nisbet and B.Sprunt. 18th March 1979.

The climb follows a line just to the right of the previous route to the overhangs. These are gained by a rightward traverse and turned on the right using aid to reach easier ground.

Right-hand Route   900ft   Grade VI*   5-8 hours.
R.Carrington and A.Rouse. March 1972.

To the right of the prominent ridge is a large slabby corner. Climb the corner and gain the easier angled upper section of the buttress with difficulty. Slabs and grooves lead to the North East Buttress.

Minus Two Buttress   900ft   Grade V   4-6 hours.
B. Dunn, C Higgins and D. McArthur. 5th March 1974.

Start 40ft. to the left of Minus Two Gully and go up an icefall then right to an open book corner. Climb all of the corner to a snow crest. Traverse a snow ramp leftwards and climb an iced gully line to the North East Buttress.

Minus Two Gully   900ft   Grade V***   3-5 hours.
J. Marshall, J. Stenhouse and D. Haston 11th Feb 1959.

A fine climb when in condition. A long pitch of snow and ice leads to a belay below an overhang. Avoid the overhang by a

30

THE MINUS AND ORION FACES

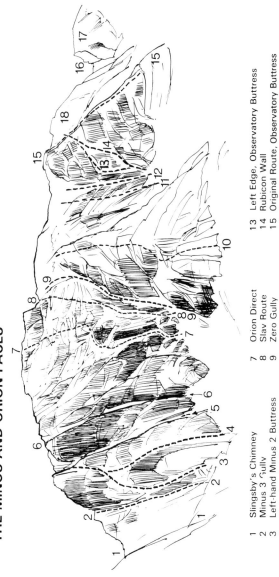

1 Slingsby's Chimney
2 Minus 3 Gully
3 Left-hand Minus 2 Buttress
4 Right-hand, Minus 2 Buttress
5 Minus 2 Gully
6 Minus 1 Gully

7 Orion Direct
8 Slav Route
9 Zero Gully
10 Observatory Ridge
11 Pointless
12 Pointfive Gully

13 Left Edge, Observatory Buttress
14 Rubicon Wall
15 Original Route, Observatory Buttress
16 Gardyloo Gully
17 Gardyloo Buttress
18 Indicator Wall

31

detour to the left and regain the upper chimneys leading to the North East Buttress.

MINUS ONE BUTTRESS

The narrow buttress to the right of Minus Two Gully and bounded on its right by Minus One Gully.

Minus One Buttress   1,000ft   Grade VI**   8 hours
N. Muir and A. Paul. 5th April 1977.
Start at the centre of the buttress, at a corner, and follow the easiest line to the overhangs at 300ft. Move across rightwards and follow the buttress, fairly close to Minus One Gully to the North East Buttress.

Minus One Gully   1,000ft   Grade V/VI**   5 hours.
K. Crocket and C. Stead. 1974
The hardest of the Nevis gullies. Easy climbing leads to an ice wall giving access to a cave below the main overhang. Avoid the overhang on the left before regaining the gully above. Continue past a snow bay to the North East Buttress

THE ORION FACE

The Orion Face is obvious: it starts from a narrow base and widens in a fairly regular wedge shape bounded on its right by Zero Gully. At half height is the prominent snow patch, The Basin.

Astronomy   1,000ft   Grade VI*   6-8 hours.
H. MacInnes, A. Fyffe and K. Spence. March 1970
Start about 50ft. to the right of Minus One Gully and climb twin cracks to leftward slanting snow patches. These snow patches lead to a groove. Climb the groove and go right to a large corner. Up the corner then move right then back left by walls and grooves. Skirt left below the upper rocks and escape by descending into the top of Minus One Gully.

Smith-Holt Route   1,200ft   Grade V*   3-5 hours.
R.Smith and R.Holt. January 1959.
Less popular than the Direct but usually more difficult.
Climb iced slabs and leftward facing corners directly to The
Basin. An obvious chimney, Epsilon Chimney, rises leftwards
from here and is used to gain the North East Buttress.

Astral Highway   800ft   Grade VI**   6-8 hours.
C.Higgins and A.Kimber. 28th Dec 1976.
A leftward slanting direct finish from The Basin starting at
the top of The Basin, left of centre at the groove right of
Epsilon Chimney. Gain the groove and climb it and successive
grooves to reach the North East Buttress above the 40ft.
corner.

Journey into Space   800ft   Grade VI**   6-8 hours
A.Kimber and C.Higgins. 8th March 1980.

Start midway between Astral Highway and Second Slab Rib.
Climb directly to the right of a short corner where a delicate
traverse gives easier climbing. Climb diagonally leftwards by
an obvious iced slab until a break right can be made onto the
upper section of the wall. Climb slab, move right beneath
overhang then by groove direct, climbing occasional bulge
until right end of prominent snowfield is reached. Move
diagonally left up snowfield and climb obvious corner to
finish.

Orion Direct   1,400ft   Grade V***   2-4 hours.
R.Smith and J.Marshall. 13th Feb 1960.

A classic: the technical difficulty is often low but in such
conditions belays are usually poor. Climb to the left end of a
broad ledge stretching out from Zero Gully and take a steep
chimney line above until an upward traverse left leads to The
Basin. It is possible to continue direct to The Basin from the
chimney but harder. Move up rightwards to an obvious rock
rib (Second Slab Rib) and take this by the face to the right, or
by a longer traverse right below the face. Trend up leftwards

to finish by steep chimneys.

Slav Route   1.400ft   Grade V/VI   4-5 hours
D.Lang and N.Quinn. 23rd March, 1974.

Takes a line just to the left of Zero Gully, but completely independent. An obvious icefall at 150ft. is usually avoided to the left but may be climbed with difficulty. Near the top an exit can be made into Zero Gully but a line slightly leftwards is taken.

Zero Gully   1,000ft   Grade V***   2-3 hours.
H.MacInnes, A.Nicol and T.Patey. 18th Feb 1957.

The easiest but most serious of the big three classics: the lack of belays meriting the V grade. Climb the gully to a stance below a left facing chimney to the left of the main gully.Ascend the chimney then traverse right to an ampitheatre in the gully. Take the narrow gully above to easy ground by a long pitch.

OBSERVATORY RIDGE

The ridge itself is the narrow buttress to the right of Zero Gully but as an area is taken to stretch to Point Five Gully.

East Face   600ft   Grade IV   3-4 hours.
B.Dunn and C.Higgins. 3rd March 1974.

Seen from Zero Gully, the left side of Observatory Ridge is split by a line of grooves which give the route, until they merge into the ridge itself.

Silverside   400ft   Grade IV   3 hours.
B.Dunn and D.Gardner. 17th April 1977.

Start 50ft. below East Face and move up rightwards over snow and iced grooves to the left end of a large ledge. Traverse left and climb left slanting line to a snow bay and easier ground.

Observatory Ridge   1,300ft   Grade III/IV***   3-5 hours.
H.Raeburn, F.Goggs and W.Mounsey. April 1920.

The finest and most difficult of the classic ridges, the line of
the route generally follows the crest of the ridge. The lowest
buttress normally gives the most serious problems. The easiest
line is to gain a shelf on the left flank and about one third of
the way up this buttress and then work obliquely rightwards
to the crest. Above this difficulties can be turned and the
upper part of Zero Gully is often taken for the final 500ft.

Abacus   400ft   Grade IV   3-4 hours.
N.Muir and A.Paul. 27th Nov 1977.

The route climbs the obvious bow-shaped chimney groove in
the middle of the face between Observatory Ridge and
Hadrian's Wall to reach the ridge.

Antonine Wall   500ft.   Grade IV   3-4 hours.
N.Muir and A.Paul. 3rd Dec 1977.

Just right of Abacus is a steep ice-filled groove leading to a
slab capped by a huge roof. Climb the groove to below the
roof and move right over slabs to a snow groove leading to
the crest.

West Face Direct   1,000ft   Grade IV/V   4 hours
D.Knowles and party. 1974.

Start just left of the ice smear of Hadrian's Wall, and climb
over slabby mixed ground to an obvious pointed block. Move
left and finish by a steep ice-pillar to Observatory Ridge.

Hadrian's Wall   1,000ft   Grade IV**   2-4 hours.
M.Geddes and G.Little. April 1971.

Between Observatory Ridge and Point Five Gully is a very
obvious ice-smear. Nowhere steep, this popular climb is
rather poorly protected lower down. Climb the smear in two
or three pitches to a chimney with good belay. Take the
chimney to a snow patch and finish with another long pitch.

Sickle 1,000ft Grade V* 3-5 hours.
B.Hall and M.Geddes. Dec 1977.

Start to the right of Hadrian's Wall and move up leftwards to climb a groove parallel with, and close to, Hadrian's Wall; then go back right to continue by a steep ice corner to join Hadrian's Wall at the snow patch.

Galactic Hitchhiker 1,000ft Grade VI** 6-8 hours.
M.Geddes and C.Higgins. 14th April 1978.

The main feature of the climb is the big rightward stepped corner system between Hadrian's Wall and Point Five Gully. Climb a slab near a faint corner groove directly below a prominent pointed block which sits at the top of the slabs. An easier start climbs nearer to Sickle and traverses right to the pointed block. Thereafter follow the corner system, taking the initial corner by the wall to its right.

Pointless 1,000ft Grade VI* 6-8 hours.
G.Smith and N.Banks. 19th Feb 1978.

A serious route following the slabs between Hadrian's Wall and Point Five Gully. Start just left ot Point Five Gully and climb slabs and ribs to the obvious slab. The slab is followed to steep corners leading to easier ground.

Interstellar Overdrive 1,000ft Grade VI 6-8 hours.
I.Kennedy and R.Anderson. March 1980.

Another serious route following a line to the left of, and very close to, Point Five Gully starting at the foot of Point Five Gully and taking iced slabs and grooves.

Point Five Gully 1,000ft Grade V*** 2-4 hours.
I Clough, D.Pipes, R.Shaw and J.Alexander.
12-16th Jan 1959.

Probably the most popular of the hardest routes: difficulties lie in the first half of the gully. Belays usually good. The first pitch often banks out and is followed by a slabby pitch leading left then right to the main gully. Up the gully and chimney by a long pitch before tackling a short steep wall giving access to the easier upper section. This has one short pitch. The cornice can be turned to the right.

OBSERVATORY BUTTRESS

This is the final, upper part of the great left wall of Observatory Gully; It stretches rightwards from Point Five Gully to Gardyloo Gully (which forms the obvious exit gully at the top of Observatory Gully). From the foot of Gardyloo Gully an initially broad terrace cuts leftwards across the upper part of Observatory Buttress, narrowing as it goes. The face above the right side of this terrace is called Indicator Wall: the face being bounded on the left by the short gully of Good Friday climb.

Left Edge Route 1,200ft Grade V 3-5 hours.
D.Lang and N.Quinn. 9th March 1974.

Start at the foot of Point Five Gully and climb a rib to a snow patch. Climb the left-hand groove above then move up right to an ice-fall which is followed to the terrace. Move right along the terrace and finish by the Ordinary Route.

Rubicon Wall 1,000ft Grade V* 3-4 hours.
N.Muir and A.Paul. 14th April 1977.

Start about 50ft. right of Left Edge Route and take a more or less direct line up to the terrace. Finish as for Left Edge Route.

Direct Route 1,000ft Grade IV 3-4 hours.
D.Stewart and W.Foster. 23rd March 1952.

Ascend rightwards on snow patches and short walls, starting not far to the right of Rubicon Wall, to join the Ordinary Route above its main difficulties.

Ordinary Route 700ft Grade IV* 3 hours.
J.Marshall and R.Smith. Feb 1960.

Start well to the right of Direct Route below a chimney some way up the buttress. Climb the buttress by a shallow depression to reach the chimney which usually gives the crux. From the terrace above the chimney go up leftwards to gain the final easy crest.

North West Face   500ft   Grade IV   2 hours
K.Crocket and C.Stead. 21st March 1975.

Start halfway up the right hand side of the buttress at a bay and follow a chimney line leading to Indicator Wall.

INDICATOR WALL

As described in the introduction to Observatory Buttress, Indicator Wall lies above the terrace cutting the upper part of Observatory Buttress, bounded on the left by the upper gullies of Good Friday climb and on the right by Gardyloo Gully.

Good Friday Climb   500ft   Grade III**   1½ hours.
G.Macphee, R.Lovel, H.Shepherd and D.Edwards.
7th April 1939.

Start below Gardyloo Gully and traverse left along the snow shelf until a gully can be followed for 250 feet until it is blocked by a wall. Go right then back left up another gully to the plateau.

Indicator Wall   600ft   Grade IV/V*   3 hours.
G.Smith and T.King. Feb 1975.

About 100ft. right of the gully of Good Friday is an obvious icefall, on the left side of the buttress. Start at an iced-chimney groove and climb bulging ice to snow slopes topped by a gully. Climb the gully to finish at the indicator post.

Albatross   500ft   Grade V**   4-5 hours
C.Higgins and M.Geddes. 1978

A very open corner descends the face of the buttress about mid-way between Indicator Wall and Psychedelic Wall. Start slightly right of the main line and climb a groove for a pitch; then move back left to the main corner line. Follow this.

Psychedelic Wall 600ft Grade V** 4-5 hours.
A.Paul and N.Muir. 1978

Start at the toe of the buttress about 60 feet left of Gardyloo Gully and climb the arete to gain a system of corners leading up the arete of the buttress. Sustained.

Shot in the Dark 450ft Grade IV 3-4 hours.
M.Geddes and A.Rouse. 1978

Start on the left wall of Gardyloo Gully about 200 feet up from Psychedelic Wall. Climb leftwards across the wall to cross several rightward slanting grooves to a short corner. Climb this then traverse right across another groove; then finish up rightwards.

Gardyloo Gully 350ft Grade II/III* 1½-2 hours.
G.Hastings and W.P.Haskett-Smith. 26 April 1897.

One of the most popular routes on the mountain. The obvious direct continuation to Tower Gully. Normally a snow slope leads to a great chockstone about 100 feet below the cornice. Sometimes there is a tunnel beneath the chockstone which leads to a short, steep ice pitch but in exceptional winters the whole route banks out. The cornice can be difficult.

GARDYLOO BUTTRESS

This buttress tops Observatory Gully between Gardyloo Gully on the left and Tower Gully on the right.

Left Edge 500ft Grade VI* 6 hours.
R.Carrington and A.Rouse. March 1976.

Start at the left edge of the buttress and climb the arete up rightwards until level at 300ft. with the upper chι ᵗe of Smith's Route to the right. Move across to the chu   and finish up this.

Kellet's Route   500ft   Grade **VI* 4 hours.**
A.Paul and K.Linkster. 1980

The most obvious line up the buttress is the leftwards slanting icefall of Smith's Route leading to a snow chute in the upper part.Kellet's Route starts midway between Left Edge and this icefall and climbs directly to join Smith's Route (left-hand way) just below the chute. Finish as for Smith's Route.

Smith's Route   500ft   Grade V***   2-3 hours.
R. Smith and J. Marshall. 8 Feb 1960.

Climb leftwards up the obvious slanting ice grooves to a belay. Move diagonally leftwards to easier ground then back up and right to the right-hand groove. Up this to the snow chute and an easy finish. A more popular variation is to take a higher (poor) belay after the first pitch; then to climb straight up to gain the right-hand groove.

The Great Glen   500ft   Grade VI   4 hours.
P.Braithwaite and P.Moores. 12th Feb 1978.

The route follows the steep, shallow groove right of Smith's Route to exit left across a gangway to belay right of Smith's Route (175ft). Re-enter the groove and follow steep arete on the right to snow.

Right Edge   500ft   Grade III*
R.Millward and F.von Gemert. January 1977.

Move up from the start of The Great Glen rightwards to gain the right arete of the buttress. Follow this to the top.

Tower Gully   700ft   Grade I   ½-1 hour.
G.Hastings, E.L.W. and W.P.Haskett-Smith.
25th April 1897.

Follow a broad snow terrace rightwards from the foot of Gardyloo Gully, below the buttress and above Tower Scoop to gain the gully proper. This is easy but the cornice is often large.

Tower Scoop   300ft   Grade III*   1½-3 hours.
I.Clough and G.Grandison. 4th Jan 1961.

Below the snow terrace running rightwards from Gardyloo Gully to Tower Gully is a band of ice cliffs. Take a central line up this band.

The Tower Ridge   2,000 feet vertically and half-a-mile.
Grade III***   2-5 hours.
J.N.Collie, G.A.Solly and J.Collier. 29th March 1894.

This, the most famous of the great Nevis ridges, is a magnificent expedition. Technically easier than the North East Buttress or Observatory Ridge, it should not be underrated. The main difficulties are concentrated high up and the whole route is exceptionally long and arduous.

The normal winter route avoids the face of the Douglas Boulder by going round into the bottom of Observatory Gully and then cutting back to the right above a bay to follow the East Gully to the Douglas Gap. An alternative start is the Douglas Gap West Gully. A 60ft. groove leads from the gap to the ridge which rises gently and becomes quite narrow. A short steep wall is climbed using a rightwards slanting ledge and then a series of short rises lead to another gentle section. Beyond this is the Little Tower (really only another steep step) which is climbed by starting on the left. Extreme care should be exercised on this section; a fall over the left side of the ridge (Echo Wall) can result in the climber being unable to regain contact with the rock. The Great Tower, a 100ft wall blocking the ridge, is not far above. Immediately below it, the Eastern Traverse follows a narrow and exposed ledge to the l. Round the corner is a chimney formed by great fallen blocks and above this steep rocks with good holds lead to the summit of the Tower. The route then descends slightly to the Tower

Gap, goes down into it and ascends the little wall beyond. The short connecting ridge finally leads up to merge with the summit plateau which is best gained by the snow slope on the right.

CLIMBS FROM COIRE NA CISTE

From the C.I.C Hut there are several approach routes into Coire na Ciste (see diagram). Average time to the start of the higher climbs is about 1 hour. A long bluff of broken rocks and slabs guards the lip of the corrie. On the left they are penetrated by a gorge but early in the season this may have a big pitch in its upper part. It is probably better to start up the bluff about 100 yards to the right by a shallow gully or groove which leads to easier ground. On the extreme right of the bluff is an approach by an indefinite gully or start by aiming straight up towards the Great Buttress of Carn Dearg and walking up a gully to the broad easy slope below No. 5 Gully. This slope leads back leftwards above the rock bands into the corrie. Yet another approach (the best for reaching the first five climbs) is on the extreme left of the corrie, close under the cliffs of the Douglas Boulder and above and left of the gorge.

Douglas Gap West Gully   450ft   Grade I
1 hour from the C.I.C. Hut.

Much steeper than the East Gully but is straightforward and, for a fit party, is slightly the faster route to Tower Ridge.

Vanishing Gully   500ft   Grade V**
R.Marshall and G.Tiso. 15th Jan 1961.

Start at an icefall about 100ft. right of Douglas Gap West Gully and climb to a cave with poor belays. Climb out of the cave on very steep ice and continue until easier ground leads to Tower Ridge.

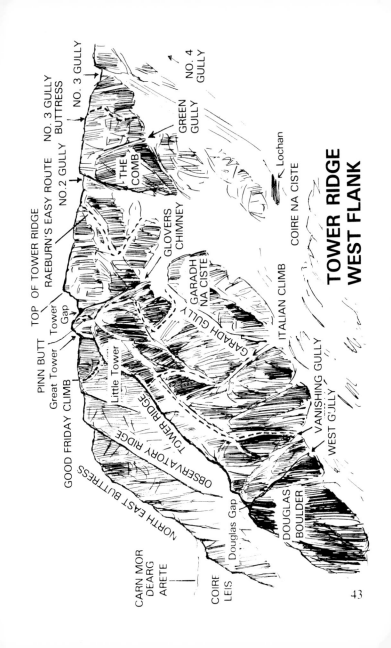

TOWER RIDGE
WEST FLANK

NO. 4 GULLY

NO. 3 GULLY

NO. 3 GULLY BUTTRESS

NO. 3 GULLY

NO. 2 GULLY

RAEBURN'S EASY ROUTE

TOP OF TOWER RIDGE

GREEN GULLY

THE COMB

Lochan

COIRE NA CISTE

GLOVERS CHIMNEY

GARADH NA CISTE

GARADH GULLY

PINN BUTT

Great Tower

Tower Gap

GOOD FRIDAY CLIMB

Little Tower

TOWER RIDGE

OBSERVATORY RIDGE

ITALIAN CLIMB

NORTH EAST BUTTRESS

CARN MOR DEARG ARETE

COIRE LEIS

Douglas Gap

Douglas Boulder

VANISHING GULLY

WEST GULLY

43

The Italian Climb   600ft   Grade III/IV   2/3 hours.
J.Marshall, A.MacCorquodale and G.Ritchie. Jan 1958.

Continuing along beneath the west side of Tower Ridge one comes to a deep gully bounded on the left by a prominent two-tier rib. Climb the gully; after a starting pitch easy snow leads to another pitch giving a huge recess. Traverse right and ascend an easy snow slope (frequent avalanche danger) to Tower Ridge.

Italian Climb - Right Hand   600ft   Grade IV**   2-3 hrs.

A popular variation which takes the obvious icefall above the start of the first pitch and parallel and right of the main gully. The ice-fall is long and a poor belay must be taken before the upper snow slope is reached.

Garadh Gully   300ft   Grade II/III   1-3 hours.
I.Clough and M.Burke. 16th Feb 1958.

Starts just above and right of Italian Climb and separates the steep little buttress of Garadh na Ciste from Tower Ridge. Can be difficult early in the season, but easy later on.

To the right of the Garadh and above the exit of the gorge approach, a long snowslope tapers up between the flanks of Tower Ridge and the prominent conical buttress of the Comb, to terminate as No. 2 Gully. This slope is the approach for the next climbs.

Pinnacle Buttress of the Tower   500ft   Grade III   2-4 hrs.
D.J.Bennet and A.Tait. 17th Nov 1957.

Starting from the top of Garadh na Ciste a broad shallow gully is followed to the left for about 150ft. before traversing right along a ledge above overhanging rocks and beneath the steep crest of the buttress. Beyond the crest the rocks are more broken, and the climb now follows a series of snow grooves in the right flank until it is possible to move leftwards to the top of the buttress. Follow a ridge to the foot of the

Great Tower and traverse right until a line of chimneys can be followed to the top of it.

Pinnacle Buttress   450ft   Grade IV   3 hours.
R.Carrington and B.Hall. March 1976.

Start as for Glover's Chimney and climb the icefall to the left of that route to easier ground in the left of the Chimney. Take either of the chimneys above and continue to the top of the Great Tower.

Glover's Chimney   450ft   Grade III/IV**
2-3 hours to Tower Gap.
G.G.Macphee, G.C.Williams and D.Henderson.
17th March 1935.

Starts above Garadh na Ciste and follows a long couloir leading to a chimney below the Tower Gap. The entry is made by an ice-fall, often over 100ft. high and very steep, usually climbed from left to right. The final chimney is the crux. The climb finishes in the Tower Gap.

The White Line   900ft   Grade III*   3 hours.
M.Geddes and H. Gillespie. 18th March 1971.

Climb the icefall as for Glover's Chimney and continue to the right of the Chimney to a rightward slanting snow ledge. Climb an icefall to a snowfield. Above the snowfield climb a chimney and gully to finish at the top of Tower Ridge.

Raeburn's Easy Route   350ft   Grade II/III*   2 hours.
S.M.C. party April 1920.

The most obvious feature to the right of Glover's Chimney is the deep slit of No. 2 Gully with The Comb to its right. To the left of No. 2 Gully is No. 2 Gully Buttress and to the left again an indefinite wall up which this route winds. Make a long traverse leftwards out of No. 2 Gully, across a snow slope and aiming for a point where the crags peter out. Climb a low angled ice pitch then follow a snow shelf back right until a shallow gully gives access to the plateau.

Five Finger Discount   400ft   Grade IV*   3 hours.
M.Geddes and C.Higgins.

The buttress to the left of the upper deep part of No. 2 Gully contains two obvious corners. This route climbs the left hand corner. The right hand corner (**Burrito's Groove**) is of the same standard, as is the icefall going up left from just above the start of Five Finger Discount. (**Rip Off**)

No. 2 Gully Buttress   400ft   Grade II/III   2 hours
J.R.Marshall, L.S.Lovat and A.H.Hendry.
23rd March 1958.

Immediately to the left of No.2 Gully. Steep snow and occasionally iced rocks leads to a shelf below a vertical upper wall. A short but difficult ice pitch on the left leads to easier ground.

No. 2 Gully   400ft   Grade I/II   1½ hours.
J.Collier, G.Hastings, and W.C.Slingsby. Easter 1896.

Hardest and possibly the most interesting of the easier gullies. Above the introductory slopes it becomes a deep slit. Generally a straightforward but steadily steepening slope, it can (especially early in the season) offer an ice pitch and the cornice is often quite difficult.

Comb Gully Buttress   450ft   Grade III/IV*   2-3 hours.
J.M.Alexander and I.Clough. 8th Jan 1960.

A large ice column normally forms on the right wall, beyond the start of Comb Gully and before the narrowing to No. 2 Gully proper. The route starts below this and climbs slightly rightwards, to gain a large snow basin. A groove leading from the l. hand side of the basin is followed by a rightwards rising ramp. This leads into the upper half of a very prominent curving chimney, the crux of the climb and an awkward exit on the left.

Comb Gully   450ft   Grade III/IV**   2-3 hours.
F.G.Stangle,   R.Morsley and P.A.Small. 12th April 1938.

The obvious gully running up the left side of the Comb. Easy snow leads to the narrows from where a long pitch leads to a poor belay. Above is a short, steep wall which often gives the crux. Easy ground then leads to the top.

Hesperides Ledge   200ft   Grade III*   2 hours.
J.R.Marshall, J.Stenhouse and D.Haston. 12th Feb 1959.

Follows the lower 250ft of Comb Gully and then a relatively easy.but highly spectacular steep curving shelf which leads rightwards across the wall to the crest of the Comb.

Pigott's Route   800ft   Grade IV   3-4 hours.
J.Marshall and R.Smith. 12th Feb 1960.

Start below Comb Gully and follow a slanting ramp up rightwards above the lower part of the buttress until a chimney can be climbed. Move left to another chimney, up this and then the arete above.

Green Gully   400ft   Grade IV***   2-4 hours.
J.H.B.Bell, J.Henson, R.Morsley and P.A.Small.
4th April 1938.

The line of demarcation between the Comb and No. 3 Gully Buttress. It normally gives four pitches, often with poor belays.

Aphrodite   600ft   Grade III/IV   3-4 hours.
M.Geddes and J.Higham. 15th March 1971.

Climbs the left side of the bold buttress that projects into the corrie on the left of and below the narrowing of No. 3 Gully. From the start of No. 3 Gully Buttress move up and left to gain an open groove, just to the right of Green Gully. Climb the groove and arete to a snow finish.

No. 3 Gully Buttress   400ft   Grade II/III**   2 hours.
L.S.Lovat and D.J.Bennet. 18th Feb 1957.

Climb up into the large snow bay below the prow of the

buttress. From the top of the bay exit right to a platform, then follow grooves leftwards to a steep corner finish. Then upper part of the route is magnificently exposed.

No. 3 Gully   300ft   Grade I

About 2 hours from the C.I.C Hut to the plateau. First ascent dates back to pre-1870. The angle of the approach slope gradually increases as it rises from the basin of Coire na Ciste and by the time it narrows to a gully proper, it is quite steep. No pitches but the final section is divided by a pinnacle rib, that on the l. being the easier.

South Gully, Creag Coire na Ciste   400ft   Grade II/III
1-2 hours.   *G.G.Macphee. 10th April 1936.*

Starts high up on the l. hand side of Creag Coire na Ciste and just below No. 3 Gully proper. Use an obvious ramp slanting diagonally to the r. This leads to an ice pitch which gives entry to a final steep funnel. Cornice is often difficult.

Central Gully   600ft   Grade III   2 hours.
I.Clough and J.M.Alexander. 27th January 1959.

Starting from the lowest part of the crag, snow slopes are followed to the l. of a rocky rib to reach the l. hand of two parallel ice chimneys which cleave the steep central wall. This is climbed for 120ft before crossing to the r. hand gully which leads into the final corniced funnel.

Central Gully- Right Hand   600ft   Grade IV**   2 hours.
I.MacEacheron and J.Knight.

The right hand chimney gives a fine long pitch. An independent start can be made by climbing the rightward slanting icefall to the l. of North Gully then traversing l. to the foot of the chimney.

North Gully   370ft   Grade II   1½ hours.
J.Y.Macdonald and H.W.Turnball. 24th March 1934.

This, the r. hand and most obvious of the three gullies on this cliff, starts (to the l.) from the foot of No. 4 Gully. The lower section of the gully almost always holds an ice pitch but its length may vary from 10 to 100ft. The narrow lower section leads to a wide easier angled slope which is followed obliquely rightwards to the cornice.

No. 4 Gully   350ft   Grade 1

About 2 hours from the C.I.C. Hut to the plateau. The easiest winter route on Ben Nevis and the best descent on the North Face. It curls gently round to the r. between the cliffs of Creag Coire na Ciste and the South Trident Buttress. Its exit is very wide so that, even given a heavy build-up of cornice, it should be possible to find an easy weakness.

Jubilee Gully   800ft   Grade II/III   2-4 hours.
K.Bryan and L.W.Lovat. 11th March 1956.

Lies in the back of the recess below and r. of the South Trident Buttress and is not far above (and r. of) the floor of the main corrie. Shortly after the start the gully bifurcates - take the l. fork. It contains one main ice pitch. Above, a huge basin of snow gives a choice of routes.

No. 5 Gully   1,600ft   Grade 1.

About 2 hours from the C.I.C. Hut to the summit of Carn Dearg N.W. Lies between the Trident Buttresses and the Great Buttress of Carn Dearg and commences below and well to the r. of the main basin of Coire na Ciste. It is a straight-forward snow climb. Above a small pitch the gully narrows, and then opens into a huge funnel. The normal route keeps to the r., to exit near the top of Carn Dearg.

Ledge Route   1,900ft   Grade 1.

About 2½ hours from the C.I.C. Hut to the summit of Carn Dearg N.W. An interesting excursion. Starts up No. 5 Gully but leaves it by a rightwards rising ramp shortly after it becomes a gully proper. The ramp leads out above the top of the Curtain onto a broad, almost horizontal ledge which fades out to the r. Before the ledge narrows, leave it by a leftward slanting gully which comes out onto a broad sloping snowshelf. This shelf gives an easier but less interesting start; it comes out of No. 5 Gully and slants easily up to the r. to a large platform and cairn at the summit of the Great Buttress of Carn Dearg. A large pinnacle block, a useful landmark, is passed just before rounding the corner to reach the platform. The route now follows the ridge until another large cairn marks the top of No. 5 Gully Buttress. A further connecting ridge leads on up to the summit of Carn Dearg N.W. In good weather this route gives a more interesting, if slower, descent than the gullies.

The ridge should be followed down to the top of Carn Dearg Buttress and then the broad highest shelf (marked by the pinnacle block at the start) can be followed easily into No. 5 Gully. Instead of descending the gully (which may have a small pitch in it), continue to the far side where a similar broad shelf leads gradually down between two buttresses to easy slopes below all the cliffs.

CARN DEARG BUTTRESS

This is the great buttress so apparently dominating the lower left-hand section of cliffs to the right of No. 5 Gully. The most popular route, The Curtain, forms readily but the other routes on the main buttress require a good plating of ice and snow.

The Curtain   300ft   Grade V***   1½-3 hours.
J.Knight and D.Bathgate. Feb 1965.

A fine water-ice climb, easy for its grade and consequently popular. A large icefall comes down the left hand side of the buttress to give 3 pitches: a long slab, a bulging wall and a rightward ascending traverse.
50

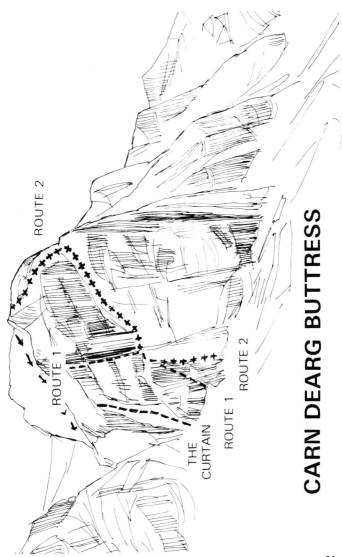

ROUTE 2

ROUTE 1

ROUTE 1

ROUTE 2

THE
CURTAIN

ROUTE 1

ROUTE 2

CARN DEARG BUTTRESS

Route I Direct   700ft   Grade V**   3-4 hours.
D.Knowles and D.Wilson. 1972.

The lower part can be avoided by moving in along the terrace below The Curtain. Start at the foot of the minor buttress underneath The Curtain and ascend this to the terrace (200ft). Traverse right and climb the increasingly difficult chimney to Ledge Route.

Route II Direct   800ft   Grade VI***   7 hours.
M.Geddes and A.Rouse. Feb 1978.
Direct start G.Smith and I.Sykes. Feb 1978.

Start just to the right of Route I Direct at a deep corner which is climbed until a traverse left under a roof leads to Route I. Follow this to the terrace. The route now follows an upward diagonal traverse to the right across the face of the buttress until a groove line at the far edge leads to the crest and Ledge Route.

The Shadow   800ft   Grade VI**   7 hours.
P. Braithwaite and D.Pearce. March 1979.

Climb a crack a few feet right of Route II and traverse right to a belay. Climb a block above and move around the corner to gain a groove. Up this and the wall above to enter a groove.Climb the groove until it widens then traverse 30ft. to the right to block belays. Go up then left to break in overhangs. Through this and trend right to the groove of Centurion. Go up right and finish as for Route II.

Shield Direct   900ft   Grade VI***   7 hours.
M.Fowler and A.Saunders. March 1979.

The buttress is bounded to the right by an obvious gully with a big starting pitch, Waterfall Gully. Above and to the left of this starting pitch is a huge flake in the wall. Climb the prominent ice streak descending from this flake and continue up the ice chimney and ice grooves to easier ground to the top of the flake. Move up left across the flake and cross the bulge above, trending right to ledges. Trend up right again to join a left slanting ledge which leads to Route II.

Waterfall Gully - Left Wall
800ft   Grade V/VI**   4-6 hours.
A.Kimber and A.MacIntyre. 1st April 1979.

Climb a steep ice groove parallel with and just left of Waterfall Gully followed by a right slanting ramp to a vertical smear left of the large flake of Evening Wall. Climb the smear to a ledge then up and right along a ledge system to a steep ice groove which leads to a ledge. Easily up to Ledge Route.

Waterfall Gully   700ft   Grade III/IV   2-3 hours.
D.Pipes, I.Clough, J.Alexander, R.Shaw and A.Flegg. 8th Jan 1959.

The obvious gully immediately right of Carn Dearg Buttress. After the first steep 150ft. the angle eases and leads with some avalanche danger to the large basin below the summit buttresses.

Continuing rightward along the terrace below Waterfall Gully an obvious gully cuts through the lower cliffs forming the far left hand side of Castle Corrie: this gives the start of both North East Face Route and Raeburn's Buttress/Intermediate Gully. To the left of this is an obvious icefall.

Harrison's Climb Direct   900ft   Grade IV   3-4 hours.
K.Crocket and C.Gilmore. 7th Feb 1976.

Climb an ice chimney and on up to the right side of the icefall. Move right onto the edge of the buttress and climb this to easier ground.

North East Face Route   800ft   Grade III/IV*   3 hours.
H.Brunton and J.Clarkson. 14th Feb 1957.

Climb the gully mentioned above to a big ice pitch then along a shelf on the left wall to a ledge at the top of a large flying buttress. The ledge is followed leftwards for 200ft. before climbing a 200ft. icefall, at first steep and exposed, to the summit gullies.

CARN DEARG SUMMIT GULLIES COLANDO ARCH SURPRISE

INTERMEDIATE GULLY

RAEBURN'S BUTTRESS

THE CASTLE

SOUTH CASTLE GULLY

NORTH CASTLE GULLY

CASTLE RIDGE

RAEBURN'S BUTTRESS

N.E. FACE

CASTLE COIRE

WATERFALL GULLY

GREAT BUTTRESS

54

CARN DEARG SUMMIT GULLIES

These form a logical continuation to the previous two climbs. They may also be reached by descending into the basin from the large cairn on Ledge Route. *Climbed by I.Clough, P.S.Nicholson and D.Pipes 8th & 12th April 1958.*

Colando Gully 600ft   Grade I   ½hr.   *8th April 1958.*
The left hand gully. Straightforward.

Arch Gully 600ft   Grade I ½hr.   *8th April 1958.*
The central gully marked by a huge block which forms the Arch at about half height. Straightforward but steep.

Surprise Gully 600ft   Grade I/II   1hr.   *12th April 1958.*
The shallow right hand gully leads by broken rocks to a shoulder and to the top by an ice groove on the left.

Arch Buttress 600ft   Grade II/III   2 hours.
D.Pipes and A.Flegg. 3rd Jan 1959.
Between Arch and Colando gullies. After 150ft. on the crest, the route follows a groove on the right then easier climbing to some difficult chimneys.

Suprise 600ft   Grade III   2 hours.
I.Clough and B.Halpin. 3rd Jan 1959.
On the buttress to the right of Arch Gully, following the crest as closely as possible to a steep wall above the Arch block. A 100ft. rightwards traverse below this wall is followed by short awkward walls leading back slightly left to a small ledge about 30ft. above the traverse. A move downwards and to the right gives entry to a steep 120ft. corner which gives a strenuous final crux pitch.

Raeburn's Buttress/Intermediate Gully
700ft   Grade III/IV*   3 hours.
W.D.Brooker and J.M.Taylor (by the buttress finish).

R.H.Sellers and J.Smith (finishing by Intermediate Gully).
31st Jan 1959.
G.G.Macphee and party had previously made a first ascent of
the gully in April 1938, but perhaps not under true winter
conditions.

Raeburn's is the tall thin buttress above the left hand corner of the Castle Corrie. It finishes as a slender tapering arete to the left of which is the prominent narrow Intermediate Gully. The start is the same as for North East Face Route; the gully leading up into the left hand corner of the corrie. After about 200ft. an obvious chimney line on the right leads up to a cave (the impressive icefall of the left branch is **Continuation Wall** Grade IV) and then the route takes the right wall to reach the foot of Intermediate Gully. There is a cave exit at the top of the gully which is otherwise straightforward. The crest of Raeburn's Buttress proper is immediately to the right of the foot of the gully. It narrows to a sharp blade at the top but this may be turned by a corner on the right.

Boomer's Requiem   600ft   Grade IV   3 hours.
C.Higgins and D.MacArthur. Feb 1973.

Above the first gully on Raeburn's Buttress is an obvious icefall leading to a snow patch. Climb the icefall and on up another ice pitch above the snow patch to beneath the summit gullies.

South Castle Gully   700ft   Grade I/II   1-2 hours.
W.Brunskill, W.W.King and W.W.Naismith. 1st April 1896.

The long gully between Raeburn's Buttress and the Castle. Normally an easy snow climb. One small pitch may be particularly difficult early in the season; climbed by a gangway on the left wall.

The Castle   700ft   Grade II/III   2-3 hours.
W.Brown, J.Maclay, W.W.Naismith and G.Thomson.
April 1896.

In summer an awkward bulging little wall guards the base. This may be hard in winter but more probably it will be entirely obliterated by an avalanche cone. The route then goes straight up. The upper rocks are climbed by means of a gully, slabs, a chimney and a further shallow gully all in the centre of the buttress, to beneath the final very steep wall. The route now goes up to the right over snow covered slabs, to the top. Great care should be taken on the slabby sections which are prone to avalanche.

North Castle Gully　700ft　Grade I/II　1½ hours.
J.H.Bell and R.G.Napier. 4th April 1896.

The gully bounding the Castle on the right. Steeper than South Castle Gully, it contains several easy chock-stone pitches, often completely covered giving a straightforward snow climb.

Castle Ridge　1,000ft or more.　Grade II**　2-3 hours.
J.N.Collie, W.W.Naismith, G.Thomson and M.W.Travers. 12th April 1895.

A good safe climb under most conditions (except perhaps for the approach gullies) by far the easiest of the classic ridges. The usual start is by a little right slanting gully leaving Castle Corrie just below the start of North Castle Gully. It may however be started much lower down. This increases the length to about 1,500ft. and gives more continuous difficulties. By the normal start, the rocks of the ridge crest immediately above the little gully give the only unavoidable difficulty. Above this the best sport is had by keeping to the right.

CLIMBS ON THE NORTH FACE
OF CASTLE RIDGE

The Lobby Dancer　600ft　Grade V　6-5 hours.
C.Higgins and A.Kimber. 28th Feb 1977.

The left hand section of the face is dominated by a clean over-hanging wall split by a groove. Come in to the foot of the groove from the left by a diagonal ledge or more directly by ice pitches. Climb the groove for 3 pitches to a barrier from where an escape left is made on aid to another groove. Up this groove and on up to Castle Ridge.

Alchemist   900ft   Grade V   6 hours.
A.Paul and D.Sanderson. 26th March 1979.

Start as for Serpent then follow an icefall to the foot of the groove system just right of the main groove of Lobby Dancer. Climb the groove system to the barrier which is crossed by the right wall of a huge flake, on aid, to a narrow ice chimney. Climb the chimney, move left then right to a cave. Go right around the arete and follow the groove to Castle Ridge.

Last Day in Purgatory   800ft   Grade IV   4-5 hours.
C.Higgins and M.Geddes. 1980.

Takes an impressive zig-zag line up ledge systems to the clean face to the right of The Lobby Dancer.

The Serpent   Over 1,000ft   Grade II   2 hours.
I.Clough, D.Pipes and J.Porter. 12th Feb 1959.

The easiest of the routes on the North Face of Castle Ridge. No technical difficulty but serious, with route-finding problems. Above and to the left of the Lunching Stone (see C.I.C. approach 2) a small right slanting gully gives access to a wide shelf which curves up to the right. After 500ft. this leads into a couloir which slants, still rightwards, steeply up the face to come out on the shoulder of Carn Dearg.

The Moat   2,000ft   Grade II**   3 hours.
I.Sykes, I.Rae and I.Dewar. 8th Feb 1972.

A great, highly banked snow ledge runs across the face above The Serpent and gives the line of the climb. Follow The Serpent for a couple of hundred feet then move left to gain the ledge. At the end of the ledge finish by a steep gully.

Nordwand   1,400ft   Grade II/III*   3 hours.
I.Clough, D.Pipes, B.Sarll, F.Jones and J.Porter.
11th Feb 1959.

A fine mixed route which is often in condition when higher climbs are not. Technical and route-finding problems similar to those on the Little Brenva Face but no sunshine; a genuine, grim nordwand atmosphere. Starts fairly well up to the right of the centre of the face at a slight bay. A long vertical snow filled trench on the screes below the face often shows the way. Nordwand follows a short gully up the face for 80ft. and climbs an ice pitch before moving left (or works diagonally left below the ice pitch). It continues to follow the easiest way up the centre of the wall crossing the couloir of the Serpent and continuing by snowfields to the steep summit rocks. An awkward left rising traverse leads to the top.

La Petite   600ft   Grade III   2-3 hours.
D.Pipes and I.Clough. 11th Feb 1959.

The climb starts about 100ft. right of Nordwand and goes up steeply for 120ft. to gain entry to a couloir. This entry will generally give an 80ft. ice pitch and then ice glazed rock. The couloir, which leads obliquely right (not obvious from below) should give two more good ice pitches before finishing on the Carn Dearg shoulder.

OUTLYING CLIMBS IN
THE BEN NEVIS REGION

Steall Gully   700ft   Grade II   1-2 hours.
First ascent unknown.

This is on the South East slope of Ben Nevis, just to the south of and commences a little below the col between Meall Cumhann and the Ben. The approaches from the car park at the end of the Glen Nevis road and from Steall Hut converge below this gully before carrying on up to the col and the Carn Mor Dearg Arete. This climb is quite variable but can give some interesting pitches of no great difficulty. Its chief merit is its accessibility from Glen Nevis.

Climbs on Stob Ban   (3,274ft.)

The North East face of Stob Ban is steep and rocky with three main buttresses. This area provides the only real climbing in the Mamores and there is a path up the Allt Coire a'Mhusgain from Glen Nevis. The buttresses and the gullies between them give several possibilities, (Grade I/II). From the summit the best return route to Glen Nevis is to follow the ridge round to Sgurr a'Mhaim (3,601ft). Descend to the east following the ridge to the col at the head of the Allt Corie a'Mhusgain (where one can descend to Glen Nevis by the same path used in approach) and climb to the summit of the next top to the west (Sgor an Iubhair , 3,300ft.; unnamed on the O.S. map). From this peak there is almost a mile of ridge, quite narrow, often heavily corniced and leading over an elegant subsidiary top to the summit of Sgurr a'Mhaim. This last spectacular section is known as the Devil's Ridge.

The North-East Ridge of Aonach Beag (4,040ft.)
1,500ft   Grade II/III   3-5 hours.
J.Maclay, W.W.Naismith and G.Thomson. April 1895.

A fine climb but remote and very rarely done. From the Steall Hut however, the approach is not unreasonable (about 3hrs). The path through upper Glen Nevis may be followed beyond the ruin of the old Steall for a mile or so before cutting up to reach the col between the eastern top of Aonach Beag and Sgurr Choinnich Beag. Descend slightly into the Allt a'Chul Coire and contour north west for about a mile to reach the start of the climb. The lower section is not particularly difficult but the middle section is quite narrow with several pinnacles and gives good situations. It may be quite hard in icy conditions. Higher up it becomes broader and easier and finishes about 60 yards to the north west of the summit.

GLENCOE

ACCOMODATION

Accomodation in the Glencoe area is all in the valley but unlike Ben Nevis, this does not matter since neither the climbs nor the approaches are so long or arduous. There are three hotels; the Glencoe and the Kingshouse at either end of the Glen and the Clachaig Inn on the Glencoe old road. Also on the old road (about half a mile west of Clachaig and adjoining each other) are the Youth Hostel and the privately owned Bunkhouse. There are also several huts in the Glen belonging to various Scottish clubs. At least two of them are generally available to members of the B.M.C. affiliated clubs. Camping is another possibility but it is far better to have drying facilities.

The B.M.C. hut at Onich forms a reasonable base for both Glencoe and Ben Nevis. Further details from the B.M.C., Crawford House, Precinct Centre, Booth Street East, Manchester.

Lagangarbh. The S.M.C. hut beneath the 'Buachaille' (M.R. NN221560) 18 places. Bookings must be made through club secretaries from the custodian, D.Dawson, 11 Fort Matilda Place, Greenock, Renfrewshire.

Black Rock Cottage. Owned by the Ladies Scottish Climbing Club and situated beside the access road to the White Corries Chair Lift one mile south-east of the Kingshouse Hotel (M.R. NN268530) 8 places to be booked through club secretaries from custodian: Mrs. C. Grindley, The Nurses House, Glencoe, Argyll.

Emergencies. In the event of an accident the Glencoe Mountain Rescue Association should be contacted through the Police: Telephone 999 or Ballachulish 222. There are telephones at all of the farms in the Glen but not at the climbing huts.

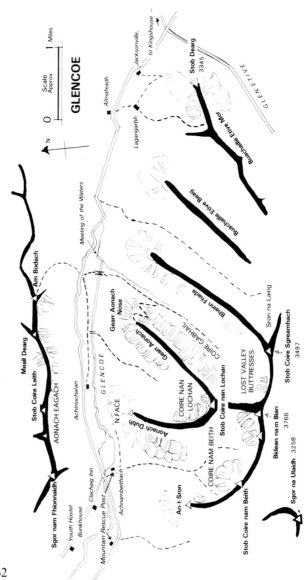

GLENCOE

Scale Approx

0   1 Miles

N

Sgor nam Fhionnaidh
Youth Hostel
Bunkhouse
Meall Dearg
Stob Coire Leith
AONACH EAGACH
Am Bodach
Meeting of the Waters
Altnafeadh
Lagangarbh
Jacksonville,
to Kingshouse
Stob Dearg
3345
GLEN ETIVE
Buachaille Etive Mor
Buachaille Etive Beag
Clachaig Inn
Mountain Rescue Post
Achnambeithach
Achtriochatan
GLENCOE
N. FACE
Aonach Dubh
COIRE NAN LOCHAN
Gearr Aonach
Gearr Aonach Nose
CO/RE GABHAIL
Bhearn Fhada
Sron na Lairig
Stob Coire nan Lochan
LOST VALLEY BUTTRESSES
Stob Coire Sgreamhach
3497
COIRE NAM BEITH
An-t-Sron
Bidean nam Bian
3766
Stob Coire nam Beith
Sgor na Ulaidh
3258

CLIMBS ON STOB DEARG, BUACHAILLE ETIVE MOR. (3345 ft.)

Buachaille Etive Mor is a long ridge with four tops. Stob Dearg is the north top, a beautifully symetrical cone as seen from the junction of the roads leading down into the glens of Etive and Coe. Of the four tops it is the highest and the only one which gives much climbing and it is generally referred to as 'The Buachaille'. It is the best rock climbing peak in Glencoe but its winter climbing potential is very limited, mainly due to its relatively low altitude. The better routes are all on the central section of the mountain- see diagram for details.

Most of the climbs start from the Crowberry Basin - below Crowberry Ridge and Gully and contained by the lower parts of Curved Ridge and North Buttress.

The most usual starting point is from Altnafeadh on the main road (parking available in several neighbouring laybys). The River Coupall is crossed by a bridge leading to Lagangarbh. Beyond the hut, a track leads south-eastwards, gradually rising, to cross the foot of Great Gully after about a mile. From this point one can take a short cut by following the lower easy part of North Buttress and bearing left into the basin below Crowberry Ridge. Alternatively one can continue following the track below North Buttress, which rises slowly to meet the 'Jacksonville' approach below a prominent water-slide slab.

The Jacksonville approach starts from a parking place (concealed entrance) on the south side of the main road about a mile to the east of Altnafeadh. It descends to the river where stepping stones lead to the square black hut on the far side. This is Jacksonville, property of the Creag Dhu M.C. (guests by invitation only). The track leads across the moor and directly up to the Waterslide. The disadvantages of this, the shortest approach, are that the stepping stones may be covered or icy and that the descent route leads down to Lagangarbh. From the Waterslide junction, the path zig-zags up to the start of D Gully Buttress and then makes a rising traverse to the right, keeping close up against the cliffs, to come out finally in the bottom of the Crowberry Basin (about 1-1½ hours from Lagangarbh).

Descent

There is only one reasonable descent route in winter. From the summit follow the fairly level ridge for 300 yards to the S.W. then change course to descend due west for about ¼ mile to reach a shallow cairned col at the head of Coire na Tulaich (more usually called Lagangarbh Corrie). This section can be particularly difficult in white out conditions. There are occasional cairns but it may be necessary to stay roped up and take both front and back bearings to keep on course. The most common mistake is to continue too far south west and descend into Glen Etive. This slope is not too difficult but it is a long walk back on the road. Care should be taken not to stray too far to the north or west or to turn west too early as there are some large crags in the head of Coire na Tulaich. From the col a steep initial slope leads down into the corrie. This slope is often in a hard icy condition and it may be best to wear crampons and to belay. Even in soft conditions it is better not to glissade as there are often boulders and screes exposed lower down. There have been many accidents here. The lower part of the corrie (there is a track down the l.hand side if the snow of the lower gully is deep) leads easily down to Lagangarbh and the road.

The routes are described as they are approached from Lagangarbh, but it is useful to drive first to Jacksonville to get some idea of the position of Great Gully and Crowberry Basin.

Great Gully   2,000ft   Grade I/II   2-3 hours.
Norman Collie, 1894.

This is the first deep gully to cross the path about 20 minutes from Lagangarbh. It is sometimes confused with easier gullies further west. Early in the season it can give several hundred

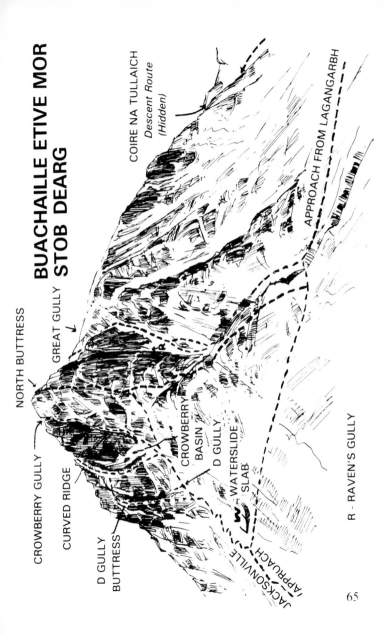

BUACHAILLE ETIVE MOR
STOB DEARG

NORTH BUTTRESS

CROWBERRY GULLY

CURVED RIDGE

GREAT GULLY

D GULLY
BUTTRESS

COIRE NA TULLAICH
Descent Route
(Hidden)

CROWBERRY BASIN

D GULLY

WATERSLIDE SLAB

JACKSONVILLE APPROACH

APPROACH FROM LAGANGARBH

R - RAVEN'S GULLY

65

feet of ice but generally banks out to give a tedious walk with frequent and considerable avalanche danger.

Raven's Gully   600ft   Grade V**   3-5 hours.
H. MacInnes and C. Bonington, 14th February, 1953.

The dark slit high up on the North Buttress wall of Great Gully. When in condition (fairly often) the crux is soon reached, a large chockstone. Above three or four long difficult pitches lead to the top. A popular classic. **The Direct Finish** is rarely in condition.

North Buttress   1,500ft   Grade III* 2-5 hours.

First winter ascent not recorded but for an account of an early ascent of the route (and several others in this guide) see Mountaineering in Scotland by W. H. Murray. This is the left buttress of Great Gully, the right wall of Crowberry Gully. From the foot of Great Gully two alternatives are possible, the first aiming straight up easy ground for the line of chimneys splitting the middle section of the buttress. After 400ft. these lead onto easier angled slopes with the odd difficult step. An easier approach is to continue along the path past the Water Slide and climb the lower reaches of Crowberry Gully to the Basin. From here traverse rightwards to join the chimneys of the first approach.

Crowberry Gully   Over 1,000 ft   Grade III*** 2-5 hours.
W. M. MacKenzie, J. B. Russell, J. F. Hamilton and
J. K. W. Dunn, 9th February, 1936.

A magnificent classic climb of considerable quality. Unfortunately it is not often in good condition and can be dangerous due to avalanches. Conditions can vary remarkably and can change in a short space of time. In easy conditions it may be completely banked up with snow except for an ice pitch at the junction (where a rightwards rising traverse is made from the foot of the deeply recessed Left Fork) and another at the exit from a cave near the top of the gully. The cave pitch will usually give the crux of the normal route (although the

Junction pitch can also be quite hard) climbed by the right wall which is invariably of green ice and 30 to 40 ft. in height. If attempted when 'out of condition' (particularly early in the season) there may be many more pitches and Junction and Cave pitches may be all but impossible with only a thin veneer of verglass.

Crowberry Gully, Left Fork   Grade IV
R.J.Taunton and I.C.Robertson, 18th March, 1949.

The Left Fork leads steeply out of the main gully to the Crowberry Tower Gap. The deeply recessed gully soon becomes a narrow iced chimney which is capped by a large overhanging block. The capstone will always be difficult but good protection is available. Although it is a hard technical problem, this fork is very short and shouldn't require as much time as a complete ascent by the normal route.

Crowberry Ridge   1000ft   Grade III** 3-5 hours.

The buttress between Crowberry Gully and the smooth mass of the Rannoch Wall. Somewhat harder than North Buttress. From the narrows at the foot of Crowberry Gully proper move up onto the obvious Pinnacle Ledge at the foot of three chimneys. Climb up to the right and as soon as possible take the easiest line back left to the crest. Continue up the crest with easing difficulty to the Crowberry Tower. If time is too short for an ascent of the Tower an easy escape can be made to the left.

Curved Ridge/Easy Gully   Over 1000ft   Grade II* (but can attain Grade III after heavy snowfall) 2-4 hours.
G.T.Glover and R.G.Napier, April, 1898.

A magnificent route to the summit of the mountain, it passes through grand rock scenery, is a good general viewpoint and gives interesting climbing under almost any conditions. Certainly the most useful winter climb on the Buachaille and can be quite hard.

Climbs slightly left out of the Crowberry Basin by any of the several variations (the crest of Curved Ridge proper or any of the gullies and grooves in this area) and passes beneath the Rannoch Wall of Crowberry Ridge to reach a final big cairn, at the top of Curved Ridge proper and below the foot of Crowberry Tower. From the cairn a horizontal left traverse for about 100ft. brings one onto a snowslope with two gully exits. The gully slanting back to the right reaches the Crowberry Tower Gap and from there a short groove leads left then right to the top of Crowberry Gully and the final summit slopes. The gully going up slightly leftward leads directly to the summit rocks. It is probably the quickest but not the most interesting way. If time permits, an ascent of the Crowberry Tower can be included if the first route is followed; from the gap a short corner is climbed to a ledge on the left when an easy rising spiral traverse leads to the top. There are more interesting routes up the Tower but this is the easiest and best in descent.

D Gully   800ft.   Grade II   2 hours.

The gully below and to the left of Curved Ridge as Crowberry Basin is approached. Usually easy but can give several short pitches. At the top traverse up and right to Curved Ridge.

D Gully Buttress   800ft   Grade III
3 hours to Curved Ridge.

The normal approach path passes under the foot of the buttress. It is narrow and defined by the deep D Gully on the right and on the left by indefinite rocks merging with Central Buttress with which it makes a right angle. The start of the buttress is vague and entry is usually made from the foot of D Gully. A prominent steep smooth step high up the buttress is a useful landmark. The first few hundred feet of the buttress are fairly easy but then the way is blocked by the steep smooth step. Turn on the left by a shallow chimney and gully leading back rightwards to regain the crest, very narrow at this point.

Above, a long slabby section gives the crux, usually climbed near its right edge. After a further 100ft. or so the buttress ends on a shoulder whence a right traverse should be made to gain Curved Ridge and Easy Gully. Either continue the ascent or descend, using the easiest combination of these two routes. This route is useful for giving a relatively short day.

CLIMBS FROM COIRE GABHAIL
(The Lost Valley)

Starting from a layby on the south side of the road, a path leads down to the footbridge over the River Coe near the Meeting of Three Waters. It continues up into the corrie, first through a gorge and eventually crossing the stream and passing through a boulder field to reach the floor of the corrie, a flat half mile of shingle and grass. The walk so far is very interesting and worthwhile for its own sake on an off day. At the entrance to the corrie floor is the 30ft. Boulder - a useful landmark. Beyond the corrie floor there are two paths to the right of the stream and at different levels. The highest is the better of the two and makes a gradual ascent along the side of the valley until the stream is crossed above its deep gorge bed. The track disappears soon above this point and the two main approach/descent routes bifurcate. One route continues straight ahead to the col at the end of the valley - between Stob Coire Sgreamhach, 3,497ft. on the left (un-named on the O.S. map) and Bidean nam Bian. The slope is easy but there may be fairly large cornices. The other route bears right keeping right of the right hand tributary stream, into a subsidiary corrie which leads up to the col between Bidean and Stob Coire nan Lochan. Either of these are good descents but care may be required near the cornices. The cliffs of Stob Coire nan Lochan may also be reached by bearing back in a northerly direction, beyond the cliffs of the Upper East Face of Gearr Aonach, obliquely across the hillside to reach the shoulder where the Gearr Aonach ridge rises steeply towards the summit of Stob Coire nan Lochan. Allow 1½ - 2 hours in ascent by any of these routes.

LOST VALLEY ICE SLABS.

On the east side of the stream emerging from the boulder field below the flat part of the Lost Valley are tiers of slabby wet rock that quickly freeze in a cold winter. Several good pitches have been made on the steep water ice but good front point practice can be had on easier ice at the right hand side.

BEINN FHADA
AND STOB COIRE SGREAMHACH.

The western flanks of the Beinn Fhada ridge and the culminating summit of Stob Coire Sgreamhach offer numerous possibilities for climbing, mainly at about Grade I-II standard. The alpine like face of Sgreamhach can be particularly interesting, giving elementary route finding practice and avoidable ice pitches. There is a rocky step where the Beinn Fhada ridge joins up with Sgreamhach. In descent, turn difficulties on the right of this section and leave the crest of the Beinn Fhada ridge about a third of a mile beyond the North East Top (3,064ft.) at a col marked by cairns. Do not continue to the Nose but descend steeply into Coire Gabhail, or on the right into the Lairig Eilde.

LOST VALLEY MINOR BUTTRESS.

The smaller and left hand of the two prominent buttresses at the head of the valley and below the middle of the ridge leading up from the col to Bidean.

Left Hand Gullies   300ft   Grade I   ½hr.
To the left of the buttress are two easy gullies separated by a rocky rib.

Chimney Route   250ft   Grade III/IV*   2hours.
R.Marshall and J.Moriarty. January 1959.
The obvious deep chimney to the left of the centre of the face. A series of chockstone pitches can give considerable difficulty.

LOST VALLEY BUTTRESSES

71

Central Scoop   250ft   Grade III/IV   2hours.
I Clough and Mrs. N.Clough. February 1969.

This is the chimney line between Chimney Route and Right Edge. The chimney (short) starts from a platform some 40ft. up and the route takes this corner/chimney, then follows the buttress to the top.

Right Edge   300ft   Grade III**   1-2 hours.
J.R.Marshall, J.Stenhouse and D.Haston. February 1959.

At the right hand side of the face a broad snowfield-ramp leads up rightwards below overhangs. Access to the ramp is gained by an icy chimney below its left end and an arete leads from the top of the ramp to the summit.

Right-hand Gully   200ft   Grade I   ½hour.
Probably Glencoe School of Winter Climbing parties.

The gully immediately to the right of the buttress gives a straightforward but steep climb and often has a large cornice.

LOST VALLEY BUTTRESS

The large r. hand buttress is in two distinct sections; an easier angled l. hand portion but very steep and set back at a higher level on the right.

Left Hand Gully   300ft   Grade I   ½hour.
Probably G.S.W.C. parties.

The gully is bounded on the left by a broken indefinite rib of rock. Straightforward climbing to a steep corniced exit.

Sabre Tooth   400ft   Grade III**   2-3 hours.
I.Clough and H.MacInnes. 9th February 1969.

There is a prominent vertical 150ft. corner towards the r. hand side of the l. hand section of cliff. This has been climbed but gives an artificial and much more difficult start which would elevate the general standard of the climb to Grade IV.

Starting to the l. of the corner, the route goes up into a recess and breaks out rightwards, eventually arriving on a terrace above the big corner. The terrace leads back l. to the foot of a steep shallow 40ft. corner (good belays on the left). The corner is hard for a climb of this standard but well protected. Above it, a line of grooves is followed to the top.

Pterodactyl (Moonlight Gully)   350ft   Grade IV   2-3 hrs.
H.MacInnes and D.Crabbe. January, 1964.

Follows the line of the shallow gully lying in the corner which divides the two sections of cliff. The overhanging entry to the upper couloir is difficult but relatively short. The route follows a steep corner to a stance beneath the overhang which projects for six feet, then climbs to gain the upper couloir using the crack to the left of the main icicle formation.

Trilobite   200ft   Grade II/III   1-2 hours.
H.MacInnes and I.Clough, 9th February, 1969.

On the side wall of the buttress, leaving the right hand gully where it begins to narrow and opposite a ramp which goes up steeply out to the right, Trilobite follows a very steep groove which runs directly up the gully wall to the top of the buttress.

Right Hand Gully   300ft   Grade I/II   1hour.
Probably G.S.W.C. party.

A steep gully with a big cornice, often containing a small ice pitch. About 100ft. up, below the steepening and narrowing to the pitch and level with the runnel of Trilobite, is a variation sloping steeply up to the right - **The Ramp** (Grade I/II).

EAST FACE OF GEARR AONACH

These climbs are all on the r. hand side of Coire Gabhail beyond the Lost Valley Boulder. Particularly useful when conditions are poor at higher levels and for their relatively short approach. However, many of them are fine climbs in

GEAR AONACH

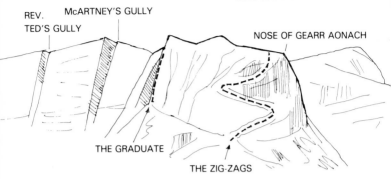

REV. TED'S GULLY

McARTNEY'S GULLY

NOSE OF GEARR AONACH

THE GRADUATE

THE ZIG-ZAGS

their own right and some rank with the best in Glencoe. Icy conditions are preferable. The best descent is by the Zig-zags (if the team is competent and the visibility good) on the Nose of Gearr Aonach (described under Stob Coire nan Lochan) but most people prefer to walk towards Stob Coire nan Lochan and descend into the upper part of the Lost Valley. They are best described from r. to l. as one sees them in walking up the valley.

The Graduate   500ft   Grade III/IV   2-3 hours.
D.A.Knowles, J.Loxham, D.Wilson and A.Wilson.
8th February 1969.

The boulder field which blocks the entrance to the floor of the Lost Valley is the result of a great landslide which has left a huge deep recess in the cliff of Gearr Aonach. Follows the great right angled corner at the l. hand side of this recess and is most easily reached by going up and slightly rightwards from the Lost Valley Boulder. Rarely in condition.

Ingrid's Folly and Peregrine Gully
1,000ft   Grade II   1-2 hours.
G.S.W.C. party.

The foot of Ingrid's Folly is only about 5 minutes walk diagonally up the slope to the south of the Lost Valley

74

Boulder.It is a well defined gully tucked away in a corner, much better than its appearance might suggest. The long grassy buttress to its right (and immediately left of The Graduate) is **John Gray's Buttress,** Grade II. Ingrid's Folly consists of several relatively easy rock pitches which give good sport when veneered in ice. Above the last pitch, where the gully gives an easy slope to the top, a 100 yards traverse to the left leads into Peregrine Gully. This gives further pitches; another cave with a through route and an easy passage below a gigantic block which forms an archway just before the steep exit.

To the left of Ingrid's Folly and Peregrine Gully, the cliffs of Gearr Aonach give broken crags in the lower half leading to an almost continuous wide horizontal terrace. Above the terrace are a series of steep walls, unpleasantly grassy in summer but which give good winter climbing. The first big break in these upper cliffs is a large rightward facing corner - McArtney Gully.

McArtney Gully   Grade II/III   500ft   2 hours.
H.MacInnes and G.S.W.C. party. 3rd February 1969.

The lower half of this big corner gully is reasonably straight-forward, but the upper part is very steep. A vertical chimney is followed to a diagonal groove and corner which gives the crux.

Frostbite Wall   600ft   Grade IV   3-4 hours.
H.MacInnes, A.Gilbert, P.Debbage, D. Layne-Joynt, D.Allright. February 1969.

Take the main line of the ice ribbon up the wall, gaining it first by rightwards traverse from the bottom of it, then back left to it some 150ft. up via a ledge. Climb the ice ribbon direct to the top. N.B.- This route is usually in condition when the ice ribbon is complete from top to bottom of the cliff.

Frostbite Groove   600ft   Grade IV   3 hours.
H.MacInnes and G.S.W.C. party. February, 1969.

GEARR AONACH EAST FACE

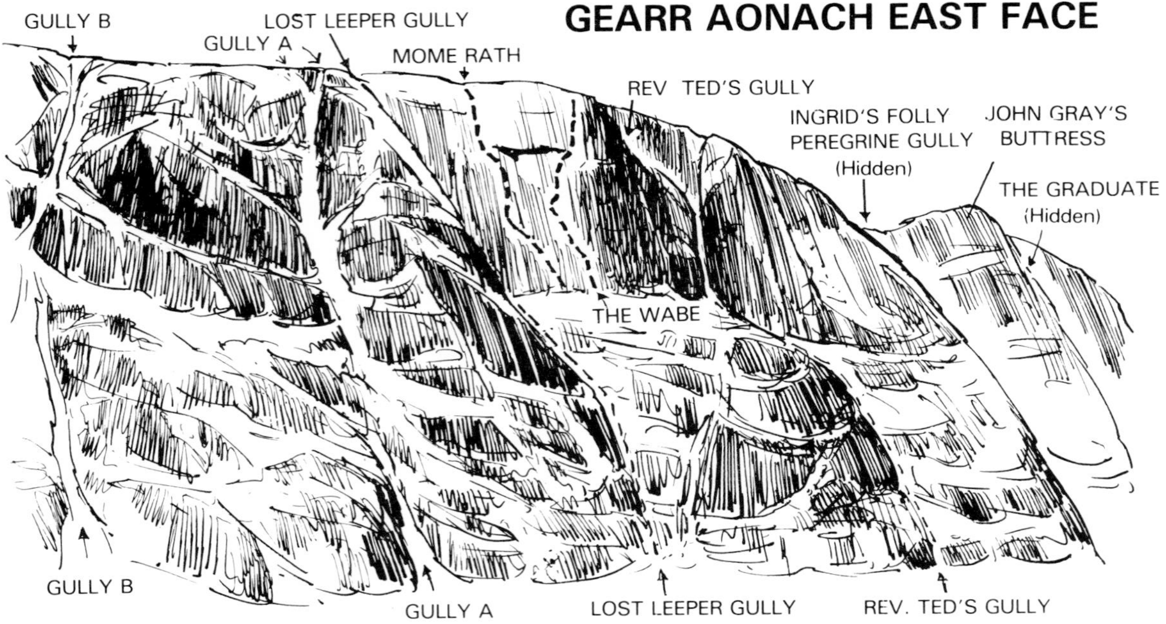

THE GRADUATE (Hidden)

JOHN GRAY'S BUTTRESS

INGRID'S FOLLY

PEREGRINE GULLY (Hidden)

REV. TED'S GULLY

REV. TED'S GULLY

THE WABE

LOST LEEPER GULLY

MOME RATH

LOST LEEPER GULLY

GULLY A

GULLY A

GULLY B

GULLY B

At the point where Frostbite Wall traverses back across obvious ledge, take the ice chimney/groove line up and slightly right. Break out left after one pitch, over ice bulge to gain ice scoop. Climb scoop and small chimney to the top.

Rev. Ted's Gully   1,000ft   Grade II/III**   2-3 hours.
H.MacInnes and Rev. Ted.

Follows the obvious long couloir which slants leftwards up the full length of the face, some distance left of McArtney Gully. The lower pitches are usually straightforward and lead to an obvious junction in the upper cliffs. Several alternatives are available. The best is to follow an ice chimney line just to the left of the ice fall at the junction, or to take the icefall direct. If the easy right branch is followed another steep chimney line will be found leading up from a bay; interesting but awkward. From the same bay an easy escape right can be made, reducing the whole climb to Grade I/II.

Given the right conditions the upper cliffs to the l. of Rev. Ted's Gully give some of the most sensational ice climbing in Glencoe. The terrace below the upper wall can be reached by the lower sections of Rev. Ted's or Lost Leeper Gullies. The upper wall (Upper East or Mome Rath Face) has high up, a long barrier of overhang. In hard conditions much of the face becomes masked with smears of ice and the overhang is decorated with a fantastic fringe of icicles which can attain 30 to 40 feet in length. There are two winter routes on the wall, passing either side of the icicle fringe.

The Wabe   450ft   Grade IV/V**   3-4 hours.
I.Clough, H.MacInnes and J.Hardie. 16th Feb 1969.

Approximately follows the line of a prominent icefall to the right of the icicle fringe. A short wall is climbed. Belay on a snow ledge above the main terrace. The route then goes up slightly to the right before making a long diagonal leftward traverse across the icefall towards a prominent nose and a stance at 150ft. After passing below the nose (immediately above an overhang) the route veers right then left to reach a pedestal stance below the right edge of the icicle fringe and then moves back right to climb the icefall where it passes through a recessed panel. good stance on the right above this section. The final pitch goes diagonally right and then back left. The route is sustained throughout and extremely exposed.

Mome Rath Route   500ft   Grade IV/V**   3-4 hours.
A.Fyffe and J.McArtney. 16th Feb 1969.
The general line of the route is a long leftward slant. It starts below the icicle fringed overhang by an obvious broad ramp and continues the line up to the left into a chimney. This is followed for about 60ft. before going left again into another chimney which leads to a bay. A slabby ice plated rib on the left is followed by a short steep corner chimney. Again this route combines sustained technical climbing with a high degree of exposure.

Rainmaker   500ft   Grade V/VI**   3-4 hours
D.Cuthbertson and M.Duff. February 1980.
At the left hand end of the upper face, next to Lost Leeper Gully is a large ice cased corner. Climb a long pitch up ice smears to the left of the corner and belay in a recess. Now climb the corner with a short excursion on the left wall.

Lost Leeper Gully   1,000ft   Grade IV*   3-4 hours.
H.MacInnes and G.S.W.C. party. 13th Feb 1969.
The shallow indefinite gully which comes down immediately to the left of the Mome Rath Face and reaches the lower slopes of the valley above the gradually rising path. The route weaves its way up through the lower crags, giving interesting route finding, and the more distinct upper gully should give at least two good ice pitches. The belays in the main part of the gully are poor.

Gully A   800ft   Grade III/IV   2-3 hours.
H.MacInnes and D.Crabbe. January 1964.

The next gully to the left again, starting some distance beyond where the path starts rising from the floor of the Lost Valley. It runs the full height of the face, is indefinite in its lower part, deep cut in the middle and becomes a steep straight forward slope in the upper section. It faces south and is hidden until immediately below it. A pitch climbed on the left leads into the gully which is followed to the right to a bulging groove, the crux of the climb.

Gully A (Central Branch)   750ft   Grade IV   2-3hours.
D.Haston and J.Stenhouse. January 1969.

Gully A divides at the start of the main pitch and this variation takes a line directly up a steep ice scoop.

Gully A (Left Branch)   800ft   Grade IV   2-3hours.
H.MacInnes and G.S.W.C. party. February 1970.

This is the branch of the gully which starts as a very steep ice pitch slightly to the left of the main gully A.Follow the gully line throughout (escape possible halfway up on the left) and take either the chimney line above or break out right up steep iced rock.

Gully B   800ft   Grade II   1hour.
Probably G.S.W.C. parties.

The next gully to the left of Gully A is straightforward except for one large chockstone pitch.

Gully C   800ft   Grade I   ½hour.
Probably G.S.W.C. parties.

A long shallow couloir on the extreme left before the cliffs fade out entirely. It may contain a few short pitches. Competent climbers may find this route useful as an approach to Stob Coire nan Lochan.

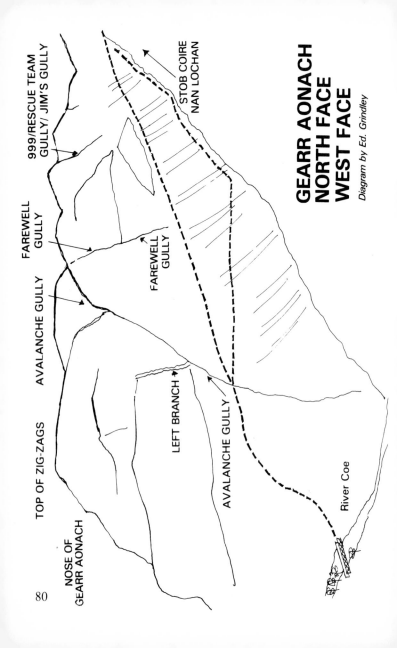

GEARR AONACH
NORTH FACE
WEST FACE

Diagram by Ed. Grindley

999/RESCUE TEAM GULLY/ JIM'S GULLY

STOB COIRE NAN LOCHAN

FAREWELL GULLY

FAREWELL GULLY

AVALANCHE GULLY

LEFT BRANCH

AVALANCHE GULLY

TOP OF ZIG-ZAGS

NOSE OF GEARR AONACH

River Coe

CLIMBS ON THE NORTH AND WEST FACE OF GEARR AONACH.

The huge north face of Gearr Aonach dominates the ridge running between The Lost Valley and Stob Coire nan Lochan. The first two climbs described lie to the right side of this face while the remainder are situated on the steep buttress on the west face below the highest point of the ridge. All the climbs are easily reached from the path running up the east side of the stream.

Avalanche Gully   1,000ft   Grade II/III*   2hours.
H.MacInnes and party.

After crossing the bridge over the River Coe the main path strikes up towards the north face of Gearr Aonach before veering up to the right. The lower stream way of this gully crosses the path at this point. In hard weather conditions, the lower part gives a series of short water ice pitches. The gully follows a rightward slant and leads to the summit of the Nose. Take the right forks at the lower and upper branches. The **Lower Left Branch** is short steep and interesting (Grade IV).

Farewell Gully   500ft   Grade II/III   2hours.
J.McArtney and party. February 1969.

From slightly higher up the path from Avalanche Gully, the climb goes up in a direct line to meet finish of that route. Several short pitches but little of interest.

The following climbs are on the buttress below the highest point of the Gearr Aonach ridge. Although short they have the attraction of easy access and a rapid coming into condition after heavy snowfalls. The best approach is to follow the Stob Coire nan Lochan path till just before it steepens on entering the coire; then to strike back left into the easy entry gully. The climbs described are really three finishes to this gully.

Rescue Team Gully   250ft   Grade II/III*   1½ hours.
H.MacInnes and party. March 1966.
The left hand branch is a steep icy chimney with a through-route chockstone at its foot. Two good pitches.

Jim's Gully   250ft   Grade II/III   1 hour.
J.McArtney and party. March 1968.
The central branch emits an ice fall landing near the start of the previous route. Above this icefall the gully is easy.

999   400ft   Grade III**   2 hours.
H.MacInnes and party. February 1969.
The right hand branch gives a series of enjoyable short steep pitches. Follow the most obvious line.

CLIMBS ON STOB COIRE NAN LOCHAN
(3657ft.)

The cliffs high in the north east facing corrie immediately below the summit of Stob Coire nan Lochan usually give good winter climbing even when lower level cliffs are spoiled by thaw. The floor of the corrie is at about 2,700ft. and the cliffs, which have an average height of 500ft. are arranged in a semicircle below the summit and the shoulder extending northwards from it. Probably the most attractive approach is by the ridge of Gearr Aonach. After crossing the bridge below the Meeting of Three Waters and following the track up towards Coire Gabhail as far as the beginning of the gorge section (about a half mile above the bridge) the route cuts up to the right aiming for the cliffs of the East Face of Gearr Aonach some distance to the left of the Nose. The route up the flank to the top of the Nose is known as the zig-zags. Although marked by occasional cairns the route is not too easy to follow and it is wise to try and pick it out from well below. Careful inspection will reveal two obvious slanting terraces, up to the right and then back to the left winding up through otherwise sheer cliff. The zig-zags are gained by walking leftwards up a grass slope below the cliffs until the start of the first terrace is reached in a corner immediately to the right of a 50ft. prow of rock. After about 100ft. of scrambling the terrace leads gently up to the right under some steep cliffs to an easy slope which is followed for another 100ft. or so before taking a short gully corner on the left. This leads to a second big terrace which is followed to its left hand end. After a short ascent, another long rightward rising traverse and a brief tack back to the left bring one out at the big cairn at the top of the Nose of Gearr Aonach. The ridge is then followed until an easy traverse can be made into the floor of the corrie, (About 1½-2 hours from the road). This route is difficult to find in descent and, without prior knowledge and certainly in bad visibility, the valley route (next described) is preferable. Although it is not so attractive from the scenic point of view, the approach by the valley leading up between Gearr Aonach and Aonach Dubh is as fast as the previous route.

The bridge over the River Coe at G.R. NN 167567 is gained by walking along the old road east of Achtriochtan farm for about half a mile and then descending to the river. Alternatively cars may be parked in a big layby on the south side of the road, east of Achtriochatan, and a descent made directly to the bridge. Beyond the bridge is a scree fan. Paths follow both sides of the valley but neither is well defined until well above the scree. The left hand track is probably the best. This comes in from the bridge at the Meeting of Three Waters and traverses round beneath the Nose of Gearr Aonach to enter the Stob Coire nan Lochan valley about 500 feet above the level of the scree fan of the other bridge. A long steady ascent up the valley eventually leads over the final lip to the floor of the corrie.

Other approaches are by the Lost Valley (already mentioned) and by Dinner Time Buttress on the West Face of Aonach Dubh (described later). The topography of the corrie is

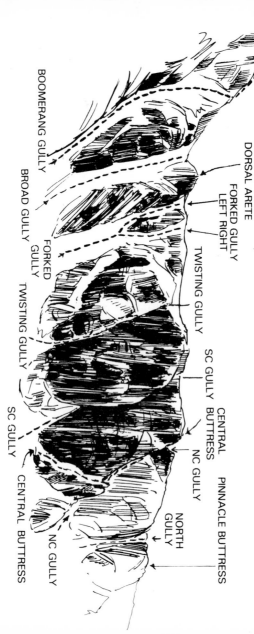

STOB COIRE NAN LOCHAN

BOOMERANG GULLY

BROAD GULLY

DORSAL ARETE

FORKED GULLY
LEFT RIGHT

FORKED GULLY

TWISTING GULLY

TWISTING GULLY

TWISTING GULLY

SC GULLY

SC GULLY

CENTRAL BUTTRESS

CENTRAL BUTTRESS

PINNACLE BUTTRESS

NC GULLY

NC GULLY

NORTH GULLY

relatively simple. Below the summit of Stob Coire nan Lochan is Summit Buttress. This name applies particularly to the steep right hand face; the open face and broken rocks of the left flank can be climbed anywhere at Grade I standard. To the right of Summit Buttress are Broad Gully and Forked Gully. To the right again are the South, North and Pinnacle Buttresses, all separated by narrow gullies.

Boomerang Gully   800ft   Grade II*   1-2 hours.
J.Black, R.G.Donaldson and W.H.Murray. January 1949.

This curls round to the left of the steep rocks of Summit Buttress (and right of an indefinite rocky ridge which bounds the left flank) and swings back to finish by the ridge leading on from the top of the Buttress to the summit of the mountain. The first long tapering gully slope is followed up to the left from the foot of the steep rocks until an entry pitch on the right, rocky and frequently iced, leads up into the main couloir. If the entry pitch is missed the initial slope leads out onto the face of the left flank. The main couloir curves right-wards and leads to the final rocky arete.

Scabbard Chimney   500ft   Grade IV   3 hours
L.S.Lovat, J.R.Marshall and A.H.Hendry. 12th Feb 1956.

The obvious deep chimney which starts near the lowest rocks of the steep Summit Buttresses and slants up to the right. The crux is a 'sentry box' at about 200 feet. Above the chimney, a gully on the left leads up to the final arete.

Pearly Gates   500ft   Grade II   1 hour.
I.Clough and party. 17th April 1966.

Leaves Broad Gully at about half height where the side walls of Summit Buttress become more broken and a notch of 'Gateway' is seen on the left hand skyline. Zig-zag ramps lead up to this feature in 150 feet, and after passing through the 'gates' a shallow fan of snow leads directly to the summit.

Broad Gully   600ft   Grade I   ½ hour.

A very easy route which often provides the best means of descent into the corrie but care may be required in icy conditions.

Dorsal Arete   500ft   Grade II   1-2 hours.
J.Black, T.Shepherd, J.Allingham and J.Bradburn.
28th Jan 1951.

Starting up a sprawling mass of rocks to the right of Broad Gully, the route becomes increasingly interesting as height is gained, finally tapering to a very narrow and well defined arete. Good rock belays and the climb is very useful in bad conditions.

Forked Gully Left Fork   500ft   Grade I/II*   1 hour.
Right Fork   500ft   Grade II/III*   2 hours.

The gully to the right of Dorsal Arete gives a steep but normally straightforward snow climb by the Left Fork.
The Right Fork (right of a 200 feet rock rib which splits the upper section) is steeper and often iced.

Twisting Gully   500ft   Grade II/III***   2-3 hours.
W.H.Murray, D.Scott, and J.C.Simpson. December 1946.

One of the classic Scottish snow climbs. This route takes a shallow gully immediately to the left of South Buttress and is separated from Forked Gully by an indefinite rocky rib. The first 100 feet leads up into a deep recess from which there are two continuations. The normal route follows an icy chimney on the left until it bulges when a short left traverse is made across the gully wall to gain the left rib. There is an awkward mantleshelf move on the short arete which leads to easier ground. Above this crux pitch, about 100 feet of snow leads to another short ice pitch which can be turned on the right if necessary (this pitch may even be completely obliterated). The gully continues without difficulty to the final wide fan and a choice of steep exits.

Twisting Gully Right Fork   Grade III*   3 hours.
J.R.Marshall and I.D.Haig. January 1958.

A more difficult and more direct variation on the middle section of the normal route. From the deep recess, a very steep pitch up an ice corner is followed by a continuation runnel (Separated from the original route by a broken rib) which joins the normal route below the final fan.

Moonshadow   500ft   Grade III**   3 hours
K.Crocket and C.Stead. January 1972.

An interesting finish to the right fork of Twisting Gully. From the ice corner above the first main pitch, climb the right wall to a belay in a corner (120ft). Climb this corner/groove past a chockstone to the top.

S.C. Gully   500ft   Grade III***   2-3 hours.
P.D.Baird, L.Clinton and F.Clinton. March 1934.

The steep gully between South and Central Buttresses is another classic and a serious route requiring good conditions. Early in the season a steep ice pitch often bars entry to the gully but, if it is too formidable, the rib on the left may give an easier alternative. Steep snow then leads up into the bed of the gully proper. The route then traverses up to the right to gain and follow a steep ice gangway which often has a bulge shortly before the top. A long run out will normally be required to reach a satisfactory belay above the pitch. Beyond this, steep snow leads to the cornice which may be quite difficult.

Central Buttress   500ft   Grade III**   2-3 hours.
H.Raeburn with Dr. and Mrs. C. Inglis Clark. April 1907.

Starts from the bay to the left of the lowest right hand spur and goes up to the right to gain its crest. The ridge leads to a tower which is best turned on the right regaining the crest by a short chimney. A good route with splendid situations.

N.C. Gully 600ft Grade I/II 1 hour.

The gully between Central and North Buttresses generally gives a steep but straightforward snow climb. Early in the season it may have short pitches. A good introductory gully.

North Gully 300ft Grade I/II 1 hour.

Divides North Buttress from Pinnacle Buttress. It is steep, sometimes gives a short pitch and often carries a heavy cornice.

Pinnacle Buttress Groove 200ft Grade II/III 1½ hours
L.S.Lovat and N.G.Harthill. 5th January 1958.

Follows a steep groove on the North Gully flank of Pinnacle Buttress to the left of a prominent arete. Start on the right near the foot of North Gully. An excellent short climb in icy conditions.

Pinnacle Buttress, North-east Face 300ft Grade III 2hrs
I.Clough and J.R.Woods. 26th January 1967.

Starts at the lowest rocks and climbs up right then left up a short groove to a steep wall. An icy corner crack on the right leads to a ledge and a higher ledge is gained up to the right. From the left end of this upper ledge an awkward chimney leads to the roof of the buttress.

CLIMBS ON THE NORTH FACE OF AONACH DUBH

The face is dominated by the huge dark recess of Ossian's Cave. The cave itself is situated above a terrace, Sloping Shelf, which slants up from left to right and starts at the apex of the approach triangle. The right leg of this approach triangle is formed by a gully containing many waterfalls and lying to the left of the vegetatious terrace walls which rise from the floor of the glen to Ossian's Cave. The left leg is a slanting grassy ramp topped by cliffs which are split by a huge Y-shaped gully, Findlay's Gulch. The main climbs lie on

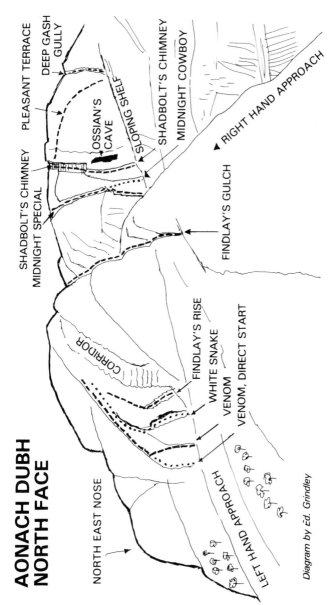

AONACH DUBH
NORTH FACE

DEEP GASH GULLY

PLEASANT TERRACE

SHADBOLT'S CHIMNEY

MIDNIGHT COWBOY

RIGHT HAND APPROACH

SLOPING SHELF

OSSIAN'S CAVE

SHADBOLT'S CHIMNEY

MIDNIGHT SPECIAL

FINDLAY'S GULCH

CORRIDOR

FINDLAY'S RISE

WHITE SNAKE

VENOM

VENOM, DIRECT START

LEFT HAND APPROACH

NORTH EAST NOSE

Diagram by ed. Grindley

89

either side of Findlay's Gulch but to the left of Ossian's Cave. The path up the right side of the triangle is often icy, so the recommended approach is along the grassy ramp (as the climbs are described) after crossing the River Coe as for the direct walk in to Stob Coire nan Lochan.

To the left of the huge Y-gully to the left of Ossian's Cave is a broad grassy corridor which slants up right into the top of the gully. The ice fall of Findlay's Rise starts at the foot of this corridor and rises on the left wall.

Venom   800ft   Grade IV/V ** 4-6 hours.
R.Anderson, D.Brown, M.Duff and A.McAllister. Jan 1979

Start about 100ft. left of Findlay's Rise below a steep chimney in the initial buttress. Climb the long chimney to trees and move left to gain and climb the gully left of **White Snake**. To the left of the initial pitch is a less obvious chimney which can be taken as a direct start to the main gully.

White Snake   800ft   Grade IV** 3-5 hours.
R.Anderson, A.McAllister, D.Brown and M.Duff. Jan '79.
Climb the ice-fall just to the left of the ice-fall of Findlay's Rise to a cave formed by a huge block. Follow a left slanting ramp then more easily up a gully to a roof. Traverse left to avoid the roof, regain the gully and continue to the top.

Findlay's Rise   800ft   Grade IV** 3 hours.
I.Nicholson and party, 1978.
Start at the ice-fall at the foot of the left wall of the corridor. A fine water-ice climb. Move steeply left onto the foot of the ice and climb less steeply to a small cave and belay. A long pitch leads to the top of the ice-fall from where mixed ground gives access to the summit.

Findlay's Gulch   800ft   Grade III* 2 hours.
H.MacInnes and C.Williamson. February 1979.
Above and slightly to the left of the apex of the approach

triangle is a huge Y-gully. An unusual route, not as hard as it looks. Climb above the path to gain the gully at 40ft. Easy ground leads to an ice wall going left to a cave. The upper section of the gully is gained by a through route leading to an easy exit.

Midnight Special   900ft   Grade IV*   3-4 hours.
I.Clough, D.Knowles and J.McArtney. 1969.

The prominent depression to the left of Ossian's Cave starting just up to the right from the apex of the approach triangle. From the bottom of the depression climb a steep pitch (crux) to reach shallow gully. Climb this and bear left to reach the summit slopes or finish directly by the line of the depression. A variation start **(The Midnight Cowboy)** of two pitches can be made up the steep ice wall just to the right of the normal start. It leads to the depression and is Grade IV.

Shadbolt's Chimney   900ft   Grade IV   3-4 hours.
D. and R.Goldie. February 13th 1955.

A deep chimney goes up from Sloping Shelf to the right of Midnight Cowboy start and not far below and to the left of Ossian's Cave. This gives the first 150ft. of the climb. The route then uses the grassy buttress on the right to avoid a loose section before a difficult 30ft. chimney leads on to an amphitheatre on the direct finish of Midnight Special. Finish up this. Rarely in condition.

Pleasant Terrace   800ft   Grade III*   3 hours.
J.McArtney, I.Clough and party. January 14th, 1969.

This climb and Deep-Gash Gully both start from the upper right hand end of Sloping Shelf. The Shelf itself may give difficulty in icy conditions and the best route may be to cross the gully to gain the ridge on the right. Deep-gash Gully is obvious - immediately above the end of the Shelf. The entry pitches to gain the start of Pleasant Terrace proper start from a bay to the left of Deep-gash Gully and consists of two pitches. The 'Terrace', which soon narrows to a thin and sensational ledge leads horizontally left for several hundred feet. After a slight descent the ledge broadens again below a deep chimney. Climb this with difficulty to the top.

Deep-gash Gully   200ft   Grade III/IV
J.Cunningham and M.Noon. 24th Feb 1957.
This short gully at the top of Sloping Shelf can give a hard, technical problem but often banks out with snow.

CLIMBS ON THE WEST FACE
OF AONACH DUBH

The west face of Aonach Dubh which faces Clachaig Inn is a vast and complex series of buttresses and gullies. If the snow level is low the face comes quickly into condition and so provides one of the popular cliffs in the Glen. The buttresses are split horizontally into three tiers by Middle Ledge (between the lowest and middle tiers) and The Rake (between middle and upper tiers). Splitting the face vertically are six main gullies numbered from left to right and there are two scoops which split the main mass of the middle tier. The best approach is to cross the wall at the west end of the bridge on the main road at Clachaig road end and walk up to the right of the stream until above the waterfalls. Cross the stream and gain access to the climbs. The safest descent is to go down into lower Stob Coire nan Lochan or into Stob Coire nam Beith but the quickest way, in good visibility, is by the easy upper part of No.2 Gully and the lower part of Dinner-time Buttress.

Dinner-time Buttress   Grade I   1½-2hours.

Lies on the left hand side of the face below the col between the Nose of Aonach Dubh and Stob Coire nan Lochan. It is defined by the vague No.1 Gully on the left and by the deep water-course of No.2 Gully on the right. Except for the final few hundred feet it is mainly grass with short sections of scrambling. Can be used to approach the climbs on Stob Coire nan Lochan.

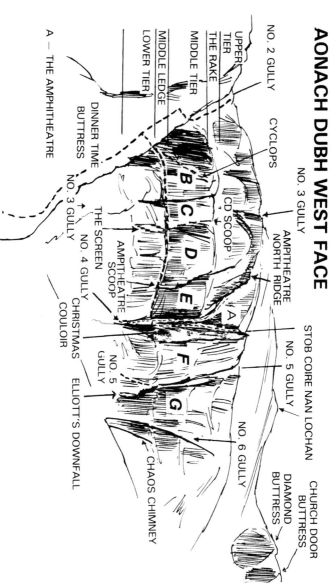

AONACH DUBH WEST FACE

NO. 2 GULLY

UPPER TIER
THE RAKE
MIDDLE TIER
MIDDLE LEDGE
LOWER TIER

DINNER TIME
BUTTRESS

NO. 3 GULLY

A — THE AMPHITHEATRE

CYCLOPS

CD SCOOP

B

C

D

E

THE SCREEN

AMPITHEATRE
SCOOP

NO. 4 GULLY

CHRISTMAS
GULLY

NO. 3 GULLY

NO. 3 GULLY

AMPITHEATRE
NORTH RIDGE

A

F

G

NO. 5
GULLY

ELLIOTT'S DOWNFALL

CHAOS CHIMNEY

COULOIR

STOB COIRE NAN LOCHAN
BUTTRESS

NO. 5 GULLY

NO. 6 GULLY

CHURCH DOOR
BUTTRESS

DIAMOND
BUTTRESS

Middle Ledge   Grade II

Gained from No.2 Gully, the ledge gives an exposed if easy traverse. The only difficulty lies in the initial pitch out of No.2 Gully. On reaching No.4 Gully ascend the middle section of the gully without difficulty and escape left along the Rake. Impressive scenery.

Cyclops   350ft   Grade III/IV   2-3 hours.
H.MacInnes and party January 1970.

At the start of Middle Ledge a steep corner goes directly up B Buttress. Climb this to easier ground. Take the chimney line above to gain an eye in the buttress. From the other side of the eye climb iced rocks to the top.

No.3 Gully   1,000ft   Grade II
Crofton and Evans. March 1934.

This gully immediately right of B Buttress, is shallow and rather indefinite except where it cuts through the middle tier. Often gives a good ice pitch at the start.

The Smear   200ft   Grade III/IV*   1 hour.
I.Clough and party.

This icefall lies on the right wall of No.3 Gully where it cuts the middle tier. A pleasant climb which can provide a suitable continuation to The Screen.

The Screen   200ft   Grade IV**   1-2 hours.
D.Bathgate and J.Brumfitt. February 1965.

The obvious large icefall which forms over the lowest tier of rocks to the right of No.3 Gully. Climb for 70ft. to an icicle recess (good runner), step left and move up to rock belays on the left. Trend right to Middle Ledge. An enjoyable and popular route.

The Flute   200ft   Grade IV   2 hours.
D.Cuthbertson and E.Todd. 1979

Just to the right of The Screen is a narrow icy chimney which gives the line of the climb.

C Buttress   500ft   Grade II   1½ hours.
J.McArtney and party. 26th Feb 1969.
Enter by the lower part of B Buttress and Middle Ledge and climb the middle tier by a short, wide chimney. Continue up the well defined crest.

C—D Scoop   500ft   Grade I   1 hour.
The easy gully splitting the middle tier above The Screen.

D.Buttress   500ft   Grade II/III   2 hours.
I.Clough and party. 26th Feb 1969.
Climb a steep icy gangway just to the right of C—D Scoop from Middle Ledge. Above zig-zag ramps and ledges lead to the crest where a steep grooved wall leads to easier ground.

Amphitheatre Scoop Direct   800ft   Grade IV/V***
2-3 hours. *Climbed in two stages by I.Clough.*
To the right of the middle tier of D Buttress is a well defined gully starting with a steep ice pitch above Middle Ledge. Start beneath the lower tier directly below this gully. Climb the lower tier by a steep ice chimney (crux) and continue by the ice pitch to gain the easy upper gully. One of the best climbs on the face.

Amphitheatre North Ridge   300ft   Grade II
I.Clough and party. 27th January, 1969.
Starts above and slightly right of the easy upper gully of Amphitheatre Scoop and goes up a series of cracks and grooves in the fine crest.

No. 4 Gully   1,000ft   Grade III   2-3 hours.
J.Brown and D.Whillans. December, 1952.
The obvious deep gully near the centre of the face has several

pitches in the lower part but unfortunately rarely has its deep-cleft finish in true condition. Gives an interesting route when combined with Christmas Couloir.

Christmas Couloir 600ft Grade III/IV* 2-3 hours.
I.Clough and D.G.Roberts. 25th December, 1965.
From the easy middle section of No. 4 Gully move up and right to the foot of the ice-fall which drops from an obvious couloir to the right of the bed of No. 4 Gully onto The Rake. Climb the ice-fall by a long pitch and continue more easily to a choice of three steep finishes.

No. 5 Gully 1000ft Grade III* 2 hours.
A.Fyffe, C.MacInnes and N.Clough. 18th February, 1969.
A gigantic icicle forms on the overhanging wall directly below this gully, so start to the left at the short leftward slanting gully. Climb this gully (crux) to a cave. Exit by a steep ice wall on the right and head up right to the main gully. This leads, with one steep short pitch to easy slopes.

Elliot's Downfall 250ft Grade VI** 2 hours.
D.Cuthbertson. February, 1979.
The gigantic icicle below No. 5 Gully gives an extremely steep and serious lead. Prone to collapse.

No. 6 Gully 800ft Grade III/IV** 1½-2 hours.
D.Munro and P.Smith. 30th March, 1951.
The long gully on the right side of the face usually gives about four good pitches, the last one being the crux. A popular climb, recommended.

Chaos Chimney 450ft Grade II/III 1 hour.
A.Fyffe and party. 26th February, 1969.
The chimney gully going slightly right from the foot of No. 6 Gully can be difficult in a poor build-up. Generally it offers three short sections.

Squaddie's Climb 400ft Grade II/III 1 hour.
P.Moores and party. February, 1980.
An ice-flow often forms in the ground to the right of Chaos
Chimney giving unserious practice in front pointing.

CLIMBS FROM COIRE NAM BEITH

The magnificent northern corrie of Bidean is contained in
the horseshoe ridges linking Stob Coire nan Lochan, Bidean
nam Bian, Bidean's West Top, Stob Coire nam Beith and the
nose of An-t-Sron. The main cliffs are the Diamond and
Churchdoor Buttresses on the north face of Bidean nam Bian,
the westward facing cliff on the flank of the north spur of the
west top and the immense cone of cliff leading to the summit
of Stob Coire nam Beith.

There are two approaches. One route starts immediately
west of the main road bridge over the River Coe (opposite the
Clachaig road end) and climbs steeply up the hillside by a well
marked track which leads up into the corrie to cross the
stream where it bifurcates. A subsidiary corrie leads up
straight ahead to the col between Stob Coire nam Beith and
An-t-Sron. This gives the easiest route to the summit of
Bidean (via the summits of Stob Coire nam Beith and the
West Top) and is one of the best routes for descent. From the
junction of the two streams the track leads up to the left and
up through a band of rock bluffs to the floor of the main
corrie beneath the cliffs of Stob Coire nam Beith.

The other approach route also arrives in the corrie at this
point. It starts as for the approach to the West Face of
Aonach Dubh, gaining the foot of Dinner-time buttress and
crossing No. 2 Gully. It then uses the lower slopes of the West
face following, for much of the way an old wire fence which
leads up steeply and then by a gentle rising traverse into the
floor of the corrie. The corrie continues up to a higher basin
(often referred to as the Bidean Corrie) beneath the
Church Door and Diamond Buttresses. Leading up steeply
on either side of these two big buttresses are easy slopes to the

cols between Stob Coire nan Lochan and Bidean and between Bidean and the West Top. Both of these give descent routes but care should be exercised as they can become very icy. The right (west) of this upper basin is another subsidiary corrie which leads up between the cliffs of the West Top Spur and Stob Coire nam Beith, to a shallow col between the two summits. This gives another, recommendable, descent route although one should not glissade as there are a number of small rock outcrops in the corrie which may be hidden from above.

AN-T-SRON   (2,750ft).

The following two climbs are on the east face of An-t-Sron. (i.e. the right wall of the subsidiary corrie between Stob Coire nam Beith and An-t-Sron). There are several easy gullies further right towards the nose of An-t-Sron, but high in the corrie to the left of these is a big mass of crags. The right hand section includes a big prominent smooth slab. To the left of this is a snow bay at a slightly higher level from which rise steep twin diverging couloirs. These two obvious lines give the climbs.

Sac-O-Coal Couloir   500ft   Grade III   1½ hours.
J.McArtney, D.Selby, B.Payne, J.Lines and G.Drayton. 18th February, 1969.
The left hand line leads to a very steep and awkward corner exit before a final easy slope leads to the summit ridge.

Smashed Spectacles Gully   500ft   Grade II/III   1½ hours
I.Clough, F.Jones, R.Fox and C.Wood. 18th Feb 1969.

The right hand line gives a short ice pitch in the first section and then follows a very steep chimney capped by an ice bulge before an easier continuation leads to the top.

The Chasm of An-t-Sron   1,200ft   Grade II/III   3 hours.
H.M.Brown, J.Matyssek, R.K.Graham and M.Smith. 2nd January, 1963.

The great gully which splits the north face. The first pitch is normally turned but the other pitches higher up give good sport in icy conditions.

STOB COIRE NAM BEITH   (3,621ft).

The base of this massive and complicated cone of cliffs swings through a great arc so that all the climbs cannot be seen from any one viewpoint. The right hand section is clearly seen from the junction of the streams on the first approach route. The most obvious feature here is the long Summit Gully. The slabby 300ft. Pyramid and (above and left of it) the bigger and steeper Sphinx buttress form an indefinite ridge which bounds Summit Gully on the left. To the left of these is the region where the vague North-West Gully winds its way through the broken rocks of No. 4 Buttress. The topography of the important central section can be seen in the diagram - the unmistakable Deep-Cut Chimney, the rightward-slanting ramp-gully start of No. 4 Buttress, the chimney-groove line of Crack Climb, the long shallow ice-course of Central Gully. Beyond Central Gully the cliffs on the left hand side of the cone fall back and eventually form a very big bay. Arch Gully runs up the right hand side of the bay and to the left of the lower part of this is a big rock 'rognon' split by a narrow chimney line, the start of the so-called No. 1 Buttress. Above this rognon is a broad sloping snowshelf and the continuation of the No. 1 Buttress chimney-line which leads up the rocks at the back of the bay. A shallow gully curls up and round the left hand side of the rognon to the snow shelf. This is the approach to Broken Gully which has two forks, and lies in the left hand recess of the bay. It leads up to the left to emerge on a shoulder. Beyond Broken Gully the final bold projection below the shoulder is called Zero Buttress.

The first two climbs lie on the left (east) wall of the subsidiary upper corrie between Stob Coire nam Beith and

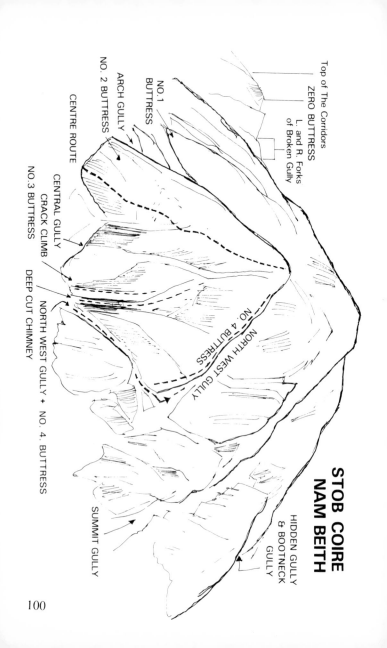

STOB COIRE NAM BEITH

Top of The Corridors
ZERO BUTTRESS

L. and R. Forks
of Broken Gully

NO. 1
BUTTRESS

ARCH GULLY

NO. 2 BUTTRESS

CENTRE ROUTE

CENTRAL GULLY
CRACK CLIMB
NO. 3 BUTTRESS

NORTH WEST GULLY + NO. 4. BUTTRESS

DEEP CUT CHIMNEY

NO. 4 BUTTRESS

NORTH WEST GULLY

SUMMIT GULLY

HIDDEN GULLY
& BOOTNECK
GULLY

An-t-Sron. To reach them walk up from Summit Gully until above a large rock island. Hidden Gully is the obvious gully lying across to the left while Bootneck Gully is a couple of hundred feet higher up.

Bootneck Gully 800ft Grade III 2 hours.
H.MacInnes, I.Duckworth, P.Wells, R.Ward and
J.Parsons. March, 1969.
Take the central chimney line for two pitches until a steep ice wall has to be climbed. Above are easy slopes.

Hidden Gully 800ft Grade III** 2-3 hours.
L.Lovat and W.Greaves. 13th February, 1955.
Climb snow to a cave and exit to easy ground via the left wall. Continue past another cave to a narrowing and on taking either exit to the ridge. Finish up this.

Summit Gully 1,500ft Grade I/II 2 hours.
The great long gully which starts just to the left of the lowest rocks of Stob Coire nam Beith cone of cliffs. It is generally straightforward. Some route finding ability is necessary but despite occasional forks it is not difficult to keep to the main line. It is generally best to turn difficulties on the right. The gully emerges only a few yards from the summit cairn.

North-West Gully 1,500ft Grade II* 2-3 hours.
Glover and Worsdell. April, 1906.
Sometimes mistaken for Summit Gully to its right but distinguished by its lack of real entry and by a ramp cutting in from the left below No. 4 Buttress. Open to considerable variation. The best start is by the slanting ramp but steep direct entries can be used. Easy snow then leads to a fork. The left fork lacks interest so go right to another fork amid impressive scenery. Take the left fork to a shoulder from where a steep wall leads to easier ground.

No. 4 Buttress 1,500ft Grade II 2-3 hours.
The indefinite crest to the left of North-West Gully starting from the top of the slanting ramp.

Deep-Cut Chimney 1,500ft Grade III*** 2-4 hours.
W.M.MacKenzie and W.H.Murray. April, 1939.
The obvious deep narrow gully starting just to the left of the slanting ramp is a classic climb. The lower part gives 3 or 4 steep pitches leading at 400ft. to a small amphitheatre from where escape right is possible. Go up left from the amphitheatre over iced rocks to a long steep crack-line which leads to easier ground.

Crack Climb 1,500ft Grade III 3 hours.
L.S.Lovat and N.Harthill.
Follows the obvious chimney-groove on the projecting side wall to the left of Deep-Cut Chimney, starting about 80ft. up. The line leads to the foot of a steep 30ft. wall which may be hard but escape to the right is possible into the amphitheatre of Deep-Cut Chimney.

Central Gully 1,500ft Grade III/IV** 3-4 hours.
J.Clarkson and J.Waddell. 12th January, 1958.
Above the great ice-trap to the left is a gully that is more deeply cut than appears. Climb the ice-trap and follow the gully past 3 to 4 steep pitches to easier ground. A fine climb.

Centre Route 1,500ft Grade II/III 3-4 hours.
J.G.Parish, D.Haworth and D.McIntyre. February, 1945.

A rather indefinite climb starting round to the left of the lowest rocks to the left of Central Gully. Zig-zag up the buttress for the initial 200ft. until the angle lessens at easier ground.

Arch Gully   800ft   Grade II/ .II*   2 hours.
C.M.Allen and J.H.B.Bell. December, 1933.

To the left of Centre Route is a shorter buttress, No. 1
Buttress; dividing the two is Arch Gully. The first section is
generally banked up and leads to a couple of steep pitches
which are climbed direct to a shoulder. Continue to the
summit or move left and return to the base of the corrie.

No. 1 Buttress   800ft   Grade II/III*   2 hours.
I.Clough and party. 9th March, 1967.

The chimney line up the rognon left of Arch Gully and upper
tier above gives a series of short ice pitches leading to the
shoulder on Arch Gully.

Broken Gully   500ft   Grade II   1½ hours.
Mr. & Mrs. I.Clough. 13th January, 1966.

The gully goes left up into the recess above the broad terrace
which splits No. 1 Buttress into two tiers. After about 100ft. a
shallow gully on the right is followed until an easy leftwards
traverse leads to the top of Zero Buttress. The left fork is a
direct continuation and is separated from the normal route by
a rock rib. It is steeper and holds more ice. (Grade II/III).

The Corridors   500ft   Grade III/IV*   3 hours.
*I.Clough, M.A.Hudson, C.Hutchinson, C.Williamson and
D.Davies. 12th February, 1969.*

To the left of Broken Gully the face of Zero Buttress is cut by
two shallow square-cut gully sections; the first ending at a
ledge about 150ft. up and the other starting from this ledge a
little further to the right and leading to the top of the buttress.
This gives the line of the climb. The first corridor is often only
filled with powder snow so a better alternative is to take the
ice ribbon leading directly up the lower slabs to the second
corridor. This should then give a couple of steep pitches
leading to easy ground.

THE WEST TOP OF BIDEAN NAM BIAN

Slightly higher up the corrie, these cliffs are on the western flank of the spur that descends northwards into Coire nam Beith from the West top (i.e. the highest point of the ridge between the summits of Bidean and Stob Coire nam Beith).

The Gash   400ft   Grade III/IV**   2-3 hours.
I.Clough, M.Hadley and M.Large. 22nd March, 1959.
The steep cliffs below Hourglass Gully are split by a narrow, deep cleft gully gained by a rising traverse leftwards from Hourglass Gully or it may be reached directly. The gully gives a series of short bulging pitches barred at the top by a chockstone. Climb this on the left to a cave below a second huge chockstone. An intriguing through-route should be possible.

Hourglass Gully   400ft   Grade I.
The long tapering gully above The Gash which opens into a snow fan near the top. Steep but straightforward.

BIDEAN NAM BIAN   (3,766ft)

The summit cliffs of Bidean consist of two main buttresses divided by a gully, Central Gully. The right-hand buttress is called Churchdoor Buttress, the left-hand Diamond Buttress.

CHURCH DOOR BUTTRESS

The Gangway   200ft   Grade II.
An obvious line high up on the right hand wall of the buttress, slanting up to the left to reach the top.

West Chimney Route   700ft   Grade IV**   3 hours.
A.Fyffe and H.MacInnes. 8th Feb 1969.
Up to the right of the lowest rocks of the buttress is a snowy bay leading to an obvious deep chimney, which is followed

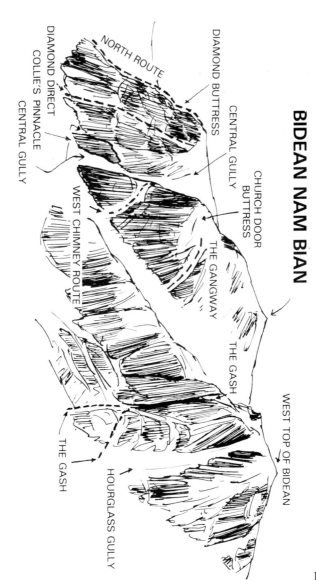

BIDEAN NAM BIAN

NORTH ROUTE

DIAMOND BUTTRESS

DIAMOND DIRECT
COLLIE'S PINNACLE
CENTRAL GULLY

CENTRAL GULLY

CHURCH DOOR
BUTTRESS

WEST CHIMNEY ROUTE

THE GANGWAY

THE GASH

WEST TOP OF BIDEAN

THE GASH

HOURGLASS GULLY

past two difficult chockstones to a cave where there is a through route to the Crypt. Beyond another chimney a ledge system leads left to the top of the Arch, an airy platform formed by two huge jammed boulders. Above a hard 30ft. corner chimney the route continues up left to the summit.

Crypt Route   600ft   Grade IV***   2-3 hours.
H.MacInnes and party. February 1960.

An unusual route wending its way through passages in the right wall of Central Gully. Climb the first pitch of Central Gully and move right to climb a steep chimney in the buttress. Where it closes step left and move through the Crypt to emerge at the Arch, a platform above the initial chimney. Finish as for West Chimney Route.

Central Gully   700ft   Grade I or II*
(depending on the route followed).

A fine route but with some avalanche risk. Start to the right of Collie's Pinnacle and continue directly to the top up easy slopes. By taking a start to the left of the pinnacle and using the right fork near the top, a good climb of grade II standard will be found.

DIAMOND BUTTRESS

Direct Route   500ft   Grade IV*   3 hours.
M.Noon and J.Maclean. January 1959.

Find a way up the central wall of the buttress to gain the right end of a long ledge which cuts across the face. Continue by grooves up and to the right to emerge on the right hand ridge shortly below the summit.

North Route   700ft   Grade II/III   2-3 hours.
J.Clarkson and F.King. 6th Feb 1955.

Skirts round the left end of the buttress following a series of chimneys and scoops which lead to a final rocky arete. Easy escapes are possible to the left. A slightly more difficult start is to follow an obvious steep scoop near but to the right of the normal route which leads to an arete on the right. The arete is followed by a traverse into another scoop and then the line goes up and left to join the normal route at about 250ft.

THE AONACH EAGACH RIDGE

The Aonach Eagach is the long notched ridge which bounds Glencoe to the north (the notched ridge) applying particularly to the narrow crest extending between Sgor nam Fionnaidh on the west to Am Bodach at the east end. The Glencoe flank of this ridge is steep and complex, very rocky and seamed by many gullies.

The Aonach Eagach Traverse   Grade I/II***   2-5 hours
About 2 miles from top to top.
In good weather and good conditions the ridge gives a very fine winter expedition. Speed of movement is essential if the party is to avoid an all too frequent benightment. The normal route is from east to west which gives one the advantage of 400ft. less to climb. Best starting point is from near the white cottage at Allt-na-reigh. Parking available just down the road. Starting just below the cottage, a track leads up, crossing the stream, into the corrie to the east of Am Bodach whence easy slopes lead leftwards to the top (3,085ft). Alternatively one may continue directly up the ridge from the start. Not advised in descent.

The descent from Am Bodach to the west can be quite difficult: go slightly right for a few feet then back left and down a gully-crack. The most interesting section of the ridge is between Meall Dearg (3,118ft) and Stob Coire Leith (3,080ft), particularly a very narrow pinnacled section and an awkward slabby descent beyond it.

It must be pointed out that there is no safe descent from the ridge on the Glencoe flank betweenthe two end peaks. It is best to continue to the end of the ridge and descend from Sgor nam Fionnaidh to the saddle between it and the Pap of Glencoe.

Several climbs have been made on the Glencoe flank of the ridge, the snow gullies tend to be tedious, whilst the icefalls rarely freeze completely owing to their southerly aspect.

OUTLYING CLIMBS IN GLENCOE

A'CHAILLACH S.E.FACE
Red Funnel Gully 600ft Grade I/II 1½ hours.
R.Baillie, H.MacInnes and party. 1964.

Interesting for an easy day after heavy snow. It overlooks the road through the gorge at the top of the Glen on the Aonach Eagach side and follows the left fork of the steepest gully. Short pitches and a through route.

STOB A' GHLAIS COIRE (3,027ft)
SRON NA CREISE
The north east face of Sron na Creise is seamed by several gullies which appear to be incredibly steep. However they only give Grade I climbing. The ridges are a little harder.

GLEN ETIVE
Dalness Chasm 1,200ft Grade IV*** 4 hours.
H.MacInnes and C.Williamson. February 1979.

This obvious watercourse lies opposite the first cottage down Glen Etive, some four miles from the main road. A tremendous climb, though rarely in condition. Follow the main stream line with one big pitch until the triple fork is reached. Take the right fork by steep, short pitches.

BEINN TRILLEACHAN - ETIVE SLABS
After several days of hard frost water smears running down the slabs begin to freeze. Two climbs have been made. The first follows an ice smear near the right side of the main slabs and then tackles roofs and mixed ground above. The second,

Dan Grade IV, takes a much thicker line of ice up the subsidiary buttress just up and to the right of the main slabs. Worth a look for a short day.

SRON NA LAIRIG   1,000ft   Grade I/II   1-2 hours.

A prominent rocky spur overlooking the head of Lairig Eilde and leading up onto the south east ridge of Stob Coire Sgreamhach. The approach up the Lairig is quite long but gentle. The lower part is best avoided on the left, but higher up it narrows to a fine crest. A good primer for the Aonach Eagach.

SGOR NA H-ULAIDH (3,258ft)

This fine but remote peak lies to the west of Bidean and has several easy climbs on the north face of the mountain. The conspicuous, deep gully directly below the summit gives three or four good pitches and is called **Red Gully.** Grade III.